T0114177

COLUMBINE;

ISOLATED VICTIMS,

IGNORED SIGNS!

Victims of Intolerance, abuse, bigotry and hate.

ARE YOU NEXT IN LINE TO SUFFER???

Order this book online at www.trafford.com
or email orders@trafford.com

Most Trafford titles are also available at major online book retailers.

Contact author Deno P. Ellis at denopellis@live.com or denopellis@yahoo.com

© Copyright 2008 Deno P. Ellis.
All rights reserved. No part of this publication may be reproduced, stored in a retrieval system, or transmitted, in
any form or by any means, electronic, mechanical, photocopying, recording, or otherwise, without the written
prior permission of the author.

All poems were written by the author except for 8, 52, 68, 74, 106 and 124.
Cover Design/Artwork by: Carlton Saunders
Color Scheme by: Niro Miller

Printed in Victoria, BC, Canada.

ISBN: 978-1-4251-2727-5 (sc)

ISBN: 978-1-4251-2728-2 (e-book)

*Our mission is to efficiently provide the world's finest, most comprehensive book publishing service, enabling
every author to experience success. To find out how to publish your book, your way, and have it available
worldwide, visit us online at www.trafford.com*

Trafford rev. 11/23/2009

 www.trafford.com

North America & international
toll-free: 1 888 232 4444 (USA & Canada)
phone: 250 383 6864 ♦ fax: 812 355 4082

INTRODUCTION

We live in world where there is hate, bigotry, hazing and barbaric practices that are being displayed upon the poor and less fortunate, gays, lesbians and transgenders, single mothers and little old ladies for no other reason than perpetrators' self enjoyment and gain. Unfortunately, our youths have to live among those who execute these troubling acts of cruelty and unfair judgment. They are being preyed upon by giants. This, as a result, regrettably triggers and encourages shootings, suicides and senseless acts of violence.

For the past ten years there have been many shootings; some that have hit home, but most that have touched our hearts and disturbed our spirits. Statistics have educated us of over fifty shootings for the past ten years of shooters ranging between ages of four and thirty. However, despite these troubling findings, the number continues to rapidly climb.

The spectacle of one's life being snuffed out in the flower of their youth by another whose career is dimmed with the prospect of spending many years of their life behind the prison walls, or their threescore shortened as a result of suicide; all combined to develop a profusion of unanswered questions that lay in wait to be asked and answered as to what can be done to save our nation's youths.

Why is violence taking a permanent seat at a desk and chair in the classrooms behind the walls of schools in our great nation? What are root causes of the escalation of violence in recent years? More significantly; what can be done to turn this most disturbing state of affair around to entice young people to grow up into respectable citizens of this beloved country?

As we approach each year of this Twenty-First Century; being a nation in charge of its own destiny, these questions haunts and cries out to us for answers. Indeed; we cannot ignore them, because the streets are being paved with the blood of innocent people, especially children.

Within the past five years stories of unspeakable violence have introduced us to a new meaning of the word heinous. However, it is more disturbing and frightening now that four and six-year-olds are using guns and knives on their parents as well as violating the right of other children.

Whether it is persecution, rape, molestation, bullying, physical, mental and or verbal abuse, sexual abuse, racism, hatred and or bigotry toward homosexuals, lesbians and transgender; intolerant practices play major roles in our lives and often rapes and destroys parts of our being.

These are the means that compose and compel the weak to convert that abundance of hurt, pain, anger and frustration into what is documented by those whom "Bowl for Columbine".

My goal as a writer is to expand the intellect of the ignorant, because people attack what they don't understand, afraid to face and accept. With words of heartfelt true stories, I intend to also prevent others from throwing in the towel and turning to murder and or suicide as a result of feeling neglected, abandoned and worthless at their weakest hour.

In a crowded room where you feel all alone, I walk with you. In a confused mind where your thoughts play tricks on you, I understand those mix-messages. In a lifestyle where you seem to be the outsider, rejected and considered curst; I share this family of emotion and feelings with you. And, in a faith where it seems your Creator has departed from you; single prints are on the sand; you're not alone, He's carrying you through it all.

ABOUT THE AUTHOR!

Bringing an authentic new voice of written word to the literary family and an inspiring new perspective to issues and concerns that affect youths of modern time, Deno P. Ellis "aka" Dr. Luvtuch addresses topics that is conflicting with the growth of respectful principals, equality and justice for all. Drawing on his knowledge and personal experiences, he highlights matters faced by teens that are most often ignored.

As one of five sons raised by divorced parents in the Commonwealth of the Bahamas, Deno's life of hardship and poverty has proven to be a success story like no other and his life truly epitomizes the realization of a Dream. He didn't spent much of his time with his father and was in and out of adopted-like homes where he was marginalized and abused physically, sexually, emotionally, and mentally.

All throughout his life he was taught life lessons, which stands as the cornerstone of his advocacy fight. He understood that education was his only way out of poverty, disadvantage, oppression, depression, painful struggles and peace of mind. He has an unwavering faith that he has been called in life to serve as an example of what God can do in the life of an individual who has experienced abuse, hardship and victimization; yet refuses to fail.

He believes his greatest accomplishment will be his legacy of service to those that are hurting; those that have been and continue to be abuse, violated and forgotten about; and he lends his voice to persons of silent tongues; issues that allows for a national conversation about the value of people and the difficulties surrounding painful issues of today.

This powerful young instrument is a gifted writer and motivational speaker who uses his talents and gifts to help fertilize this world. He realize that in order for the world to become a better place, we must first start with "The man in the mirror" as singer Michael Jackson asks us to and "Be the change we want to see in the world" as he sees himself into the eyes of hurting disadvantage abused children.

He truly has a story to tell and with his dynamic way of delivery rooted into the experiences and passion for those he continues to fight for, when you listen to him speak, you are instantly moved and inspired in ways that can only be a testament to what this young man has gone through to get to where he is today and pressing toward. He is truly an authentic, caring and inspiring voice for our time.

Although this book is not personally based upon his life, traces of his personal experiences is composed and related throughout these pages. He is a wonderful person with a heart of gold, a desperate fervor for helping those that are unable to help themselves and a body of hope for a better tomorrow.

"Hope; Hope in the face of difficulty. Hope in the face of uncertainty; the audacity of hope" for silent tongues that awaits a voice, and a country that is in desperate need of a leader that cares about people. President Barrack H. Obama and future Prime Minister of the Commonwealth of the Bahamas Deno P. Ellis

TABLE OF CONTENTS

MY PRAYER

Father; give me the passion to reach the youths of this nation,
Give me wisdom to write good songs for them to sing.
Give me the knowledge to speak the message they would need in tribulation.
And the melody that play with bells that loudly ring.

This prayer is for those, whom are crying,
In searching of a better way.
It is for those, who are dying,
Even for the parents of today.

Father, give me the vision to reach the next generation,
Your message to give to future boys and girls.
Give us strength to overcome temptation,
And thank you for sending me to reach those around the world.

My prayer is for the freedom of slaves in sorrow,
And for those that have no say.
It is for those of tomorrow,
But, strictly for the youths of today.

JOURNEY OF THE GENERATIONS!

Life as we now know it is speaking a new language; that language is the fluent speech of violence that is occurring in the world today. Today's youths are far different from those of yesterday.

This Twenty-First Century, which now house youths of modern time have a desperate need and hunger to fit in; starvation to be a part of something, and to be accepted by their peers. Like a water-thirst reindeer that is fully aware of the danger that awaits at the river's edge; desperation propels them to assume the risk for, if only one taste of life's water; teens are sacrificing themselves, their morals and their future for a brief acceptance into companionship and to be a part of that something even if it's not positive or can and possibly will kill them in their youth.

The way they respond and deal with situations is a lot different from the traditional way the generations of old dealt with theirs. Integration is very important to them, and because of that, in their world; anything goes and they usually do whatever it takes to maintain their place of acceptance.

Days gone by, all that was needed to establish bonds between two strangers were simple handshakes and introduction of identities, a few conversations and relationships blossomed into lifelong partners of devoted trust.

Nowadays; to be accepted, one must be beaten violently by those they wish to be comrades with, tease and bully others before going out and possibly taking an innocent victim's life as a form of test to establish manhood, strength and secrecy.

This beating gives them almost a permanent enrollment into the University of the Streets where they learn curriculum of hate and crimes against anyone other than those of their university, even if that includes their own parents, siblings and family members.

They learn how to steal, kill, and destroy the very fundamentals of which our ancestors had given their lives in order to allow us to have freedom of speech, peace and harmony in this beautiful country.

Our youths have convinced themselves that they have a foolproof on the educators of wisdom, knowledge and understanding from the days of old, whom no doubt, had experienced for themselves the consequences of harshly knowing the series of one's actions.

They carefully structured and deposited knowledge to identify signs and warnings into the lives of generations they lead, which was with intent to trickle down to today's youths to prevent them from experiencing the very faith that most certainly will come following choices they will make for their lives. Bad choices usually leave no room to reflect on thoughts that would have prevented consequences if they had only listened to the advice that were issued earlier by those whom knew them best.

The world is ever changing and what use to concern the older folks are not the same concerns of today. Days of old people opened up their homes to friends, loved ones and strangers alike that were in need, despite the square footage of their quarters. Once someone was in need, they shared their homes and beds with them to provide shelter for family, friends and strangers alike.

Interesting stories of "Jack and Jill" were shared at the dinner table as they communion together over hot meals. Clothing that were passed on to be worn from one person to another didn't have name like "Hand me downs", because those who had gotten them were appreciative to the blessing, especially mothers that were single parents and were struggling to keep food on the table.

It seem as though at our most weakest and desperate point of our lives, when difficulty makes it hard for disadvantaged families to see the city for the smoke, that's when hurting families are usually neglected and abandoned by the government and society. However, the second our names are printed in lights on billboards or magazines, we get more handouts and support that we could ever use in a lifetime, and it's not needed.

Food, clothing and shelter are very important items; they are vital goods that most mothers would do whatever it takes almost to provide those essential items to their children when they have exhausted out all of their book related avenues that is usually quoted to them and they are left with no other choice.

When you are fighting the battle of hunger and poverty alone, desperation kicks in; cries from little hungry mouths play in your mind like a jukebox. That painful melody compels them to do the unthinkable; whatever that may be. This is the attitude of the age of generation we're living in today; sad, but true.

I wish to remind this present generation, future generations, and the generation of yesteryear who have adopted the attitude and mindset of this modern philosophy that life is not about keeping score. It is not about how many friends we have or how accepted we are. It is not about if you have plans this weekend or if we will be spending our time alone. Life is not about who we're dating, who we use to date, how many people we've dated in the past, or whether we have ever been with anyone intimately.

Life is not about who we have kissed or about the number of persons we've had or desired to engage in sexual activities with. It is not about who our families are or how financially stable or unbalanced they are. It doesn't matter the model of vehicle they drive or what designer brands they wear.

Life is not about where we were sent to school and it is not about our external beauty. It is not about the brand of clothing we wear, what designer shoes we have own, or what kind of music we listen to.

It is not about if our hair is blonde, red, black or brown, or whether our skin is too light, too dark or too Hispanic looking. It is not about the grades we get in school, how smart we are, or how welcoming or rejecting others respond to us. It is not about how wealthy we are or what size structure of architectural art we live in. Although these are very important issues; for the most part, life is just not about these mere concerns.

Life is about who we love and how we treat them. It is about who we make happy or unhappy purposely. It is about keeping or betraying trust. It is about building and rebuilding one's self-esteem, while keeping in mind one's self worth. It is about friendships being used as sanctities or as weapons.

It is about what we say and mean; some hurtful, others uplifting. Life is about the consequences that follow the spreading of rumors and contributing to petty gossip. It is about what judgments we pass down on others and how it would affect their lives.

It is about who we have ignored with full control and intent when we sit near to them on bus stops; the ones we walk by along the hallway of our schools and those we refuse to sit next to in cafeterias.

It is about jealousy, fear, ignorance, and revenge. It is about transporting inner hate or love for others, and whether we allow it to grow and spread among our brothers and sisters as a result of difference.

Life is about what we do with the wealth we accumulate; whether it is used for blessings or cursing. It is also about whom we open the doors of our homes to at a time when help is needed.

Most of all; life is about whether we use our lives to touch or poison other people's hearts and minds in such ways that could never have occurred alone.

Only you can choose the way those hearts and minds are affected when choices are made. That is what life is all about in my opinion; maybe you have a difference in opinion.

The importance of speech play a role in our every day lives. The power of words can elevate an individual to the highest status of success by way of self-esteem, faith in self and understanding their worth and value; or it can ground them into the valley of dried bones without any ability to resurrect.

As a child I have been taught that old familiar myth that "Sticks and stones may only break my bones, but words could never hurt me"; I guest they were talking about the physical aspect of it, because as I got older and begin to interact and open myself to others, I found that one would prefer to be hurt physically by sticks and stones rather than emotional and mentally traumatized by harsh words, which affects our thoughts, our emotions, and our inner feelings.

As I graduated from adolescent to teenage adult I was told to keep my words silent and not to allow my thoughts to breakdown the strength of one's self-esteem; but to express rather, my feelings in a grave silence of mind if it was of negative means.

I do not have the answers to make this world a better place to dwell, but I know it is on the brink of coming to a close as the book of Revelation warns. Therefore; as a people, we should unit together and live as one instead of separating ourselves into groups and fighting among each other as though we are wild animals in the African jungle.

Hundreds of thousands of youthful lives are being lost each and every year by means of heinous acts of violence. Murder, rape, and molestation are all ways of which we violate the right of others whether they are Americans, Bahamians, Haitians, Africans, whomever.

We are all sheltered under the umbrella of human beings; therefore, we deserve equal rights to live and enjoy our lives in any environment that breathes the fresh air of human nature, any lifestyle, as long as it is not breaking laws, and be all that we can be despite what doors we walk out each day.

We sacrifice our men, woman and children daily all in the name of "Peace" in order to keep this country strong and free. Yet we haven't realized as a people first and foremost the fact that the enemy that we fail to identify is those sharing this country and native identity with us.

We can self proclaim that we are a "Free" nation, because of what we can say, do and accomplish. But, are we really?

There are nations with only a fraction of what we have and many don't fight wars; yet they are actually free. We have to understand that we can be slaves without masters and held captive without chains holding us. Bondage is in the mind and until we go back to understanding who we are and abolishing separation and divide, attacking and beating others, and bashing people with slurs, we are captive slaves to our minds.

We have forgotten the purpose of why we make sacrifice year after sending men and woman to the battlefield to fight for us. And because of that, we hate on each other for simple petty or no reason at all; allowing that hate to elevate into anger, generating through the ages where the skill of death is taught to our children rather than the gift of brotherly love.

We were born into countries we were birth into for two common goals and purposes. Those goals are to equip ourselves of the knowledge that was left behind by our ancestors to continue on legacies of which they had started that was intended to influence and encourage us to not only be keepers of our brothers, but to also identify the enemy within.

Education is power and I know that the governing parents of this country prioritize themselves educating their people, and that's wonderful and very important. However, education is a broad field and we must not only educate ourselves in math and science, but also provide ourselves with wisdom knowledge and understanding of knowing that the best weapon the enemy can use to destroy any nation the weapon of turning the people against itself.

We past people of all walks of life each and every day; some are at our jobs, while others are on boardwalks; some along the hallway of our schools, while others are on the streets of life. A number of them walk with their heads lifted high, while others stroll with it hung low. A few of their faces are painted bright with smiles, while others are darkened with despair.

Despite the deception of the external grief or smile, most times we don't know what environments or homes they are coming out of or what they are going through in the privacy of their hearts and minds. Because of that, I must warn that we should be extremely careful and cautious of how we treat them as they cross our paths along the way.

I received an email the other day and although I'm unaware of the author, I share it with you as it is certainly important and brings light to this point.

A young man writes:

"One day as a freshman in high school I saw a kid from my class who was walking home from school. His name was Kyle and it looked like he was carrying all of his books in his hands.

I thought to myself, why would anyone take home all their books on a Friday, but figured he must really be a nerd to do such a thing like that. I had quite a weekend planned for me, such as attending parties and a football game with my friends that following afternoon, so I shrugged my shoulders and went on my way.

As I was walking I saw a group of kids running toward the boy with all the books. I stopped for a moment to see why they were running toward him. I watched as they ran at him knocking all of his books out from his arms tripping him over where he landed onto the floor into the dirt.

They burst out in laughter as his glasses went flying from his face landing into the grass about ten feet away from him. He looked up and I saw this terrible sadness in his eyes; my heart went out to him.

I jogged over to him as he crawled around partially blinded looking for his glasses with tears in his eyes. I picked up his glasses and handed them to him as I said, "Those guys are jerks", and they really should go get a life, in attempt to uplift his spirit.

He looked at me and said, "Hey thanks". There was a big smile on his face thereafter, one of those smiles that showered real gratitude.

I helped picked up his books and asked where he lived. As it turned out, he lived nearby to me, and as a result, I asked why I had never seen him before in the neighborhood. He said he had attended a private school before attending the school we both were attending at that time. I knew in my heart I would have never hung out with a private school kid before, but he seem to be a cool kid once I had started talking to him.

We talked all the way home with me carrying some of his books. He turned out to be a pretty cool kid, so just before we parted for the evening I asked him if he wanted to play a little football with my friends and me that afternoon and he agreed.

We hung out all that following weekend and the more I got to know Kyle, the more I fell in love with his spirit and personality and my friends also accepted him and thought the same of him being a pretty cool guy to be around.

Monday morning came and there was Kyle with the huge stack of books again. I stopped him and said, "Boy you are going to really build some serious muscles with this pile of books you are carrying around everyday".

He just laughed and handed me half the books to carry for him. Over the next four years Kyle and I became the best of friends. When we were seniors we thought about attending college. Kyle decided on attending Georgetown and I decided to attend Duke.

I knew that we would always be friends and that the miles would never be a problem for us. He was going to be a doctor and I was going for business on a football scholarship. Kyle was valedictorian of our class.

I teased him all the time about being a nerd. He had to prepare a speech for graduation. I was so glad it wasn't me having to get up there and speak graduation day. I saw Kyle on that day before the ceremony and he looked great.

He was one of those guys that had really found his value during high school. He filled out and actually looked good in glasses and had more dates than I had, because the girls loved him. I must admit that I was jealous at times of his popularity.

Graduation day came and it was one of those days I could have seen that he was nervous about his speech and by way of encouragement, I smacked him on the back and said, "Hey big guy; you'll be great". He looked at me with one of those looks, a really grateful one and smiled. Thanks he said. As he started his speech he cleared his throat and began to read his lines.

He said graduation is a time to say thanks to those who helped you make it through those tough years of high school; persons such as parents, siblings; maybe a coach, but most important, friends.

You see; I'm here today because of a friend and I want to tell all of you that the best gift you can give to someone is the gift of genuine friendship. I'm going to tell you a story, he added.

I just looked at my friend with disbelief as he told the story of the first day we met. He said on that day he had planned to kill himself over the weekend. He spoke of how he had cleaned out his locker to save his mother the pain of having to do it later down after his suicide. He looked hard at me and gave me a little smile. Thankfully, I was saved; my friend saved me from doing the unspeakable.

I heard the gasp go through the crowd as this handsome popular boy told us all about his weakest moment. I saw his mother and father looking at me and smiling with that same grateful smile I had seen on his face a few days earlier.

The day I saw him walking with all of his books into his hands could have been the last time I could have seen him if I had been like the rest whom had mistreated him, and not until that moment did I realize its depth".

Friends, I wish to warn never underestimate the power of your actions. With one small gesture or word of encouragement, maybe an act of goodwill, you can change a person's life for better or for worse, or can rather, build a life or destroy one.

God put us all on earth to impact each other's lives one way or another. We must see God in others as we show Him in our daily life.

NO ONE KNOWS!

One day as I was walking by,
I looked over, when I saw this guy.
Standing there all alone,
Not realizing he did not have a home.
I turned around and proceeded to walk over,
Because, apart from blood; he was still my brother.
Just before I got there, I was suddenly distracted,
She said she needed me, and without thought, I reacted.
I jumped into her car and we droved by,
But, what crushed my heart; was the words he cried.

No one knows my problem,
No one knows my pain.
There is no one that can solve them,
And I'm too ashamed.
I'm standing here so lonely, standing here so lost,
Dad said he'd be there, while my mother paid the cost.

As we continued driving along,
His words repeatedly played in my mind like a song.
In my hands my head dropped,
As the questions danced like the King of pop.
Why didn't I stop?
Oh why didn't I stop?

As my car came to a stop,
I knew I had another day to shop.
So I rushed on back,
But met the crowd into the street, all packed.
I pulled myself through,
To see what was going on.
My heart became saddened for one I never knew,
The hour laughter became sorrow, when the doctor shouted; this life is gone.

I knew I should've stopped,
Yet I kept driving on.
My mind said I had to shop,
Now by suicide, another young life is gone.
I was giving a task, an opportunity I'll forever crave,
The moment I jumped into that car, I sent another youth into an early grave.

OUR COUNTRY'S YOUTH; HISTORY, PRESENT, FUTURE

—————➤●⊂—————

One of the single greatest threats to the quality of our lives and productive development of our country is criminal activities, especially crimes which involves violence and destructive teens committing them. The level of crime seems to be at its peek. It is statistically known that more than eleven thousand lives are taken by gun violence each year in the United States of America alone.

One of the world's leading magazines, Time Magazine outlined America as "America the Violent". Wow; what a disturbing tag.

The yearly rate in the Bahamas and other Caribbean countries is a lot smaller. However, the Bahamas with a population fewer than three hundred and seven thousand people, a murder rate of eighty a year in my opinion is ridiculous.

There is a wave of violence sweeping through our country, and I guest like myself; living legends that have lived through a few generations are first shocked that their country, this country has come to such a past; a mockery to the seeds they had planted and ashamed to have experience.

I'm sure they are also curious to discover themselves the epidemic to kids who kill. In order to do that, we must first try to discover when did this curse started and where did we go wrong. Believe it or not, this behavior developed from within the home and filtered onto our streets.

In my opinion, this curse was called into existence during the dark ages when parents of other races sat down at their dinner tables and with an iron fist; they bombarded their children's minds with mean harsh negative words of those of different creed and color. They demanded them not to associate with as a result of the concept and thoughts they had about them, observing them as trash.

These people whom shared the same blood as those of other races were beaten, raped and killed in the presence of sons and daughters of accepted races as their parents and others of the same color danced and chaired with joy to see people of forbidden shades of grey hung from nooses, burnt alive in the streets, insulted and disrespected.

Hate, bigotry, intolerance were seeds that had been planted by adults into the stomachs of children, and they did it in the most violent and demeaning way. They felt as though people of other creed and color were not good enough to get a qualified education; therefore, they robbed them of it so that they can remain as the ignorant dense symbol they had portrayed them to be. As a result of this, most of these teen girls, without an education, became dependent upon men who were bringing in a paycheck.

Little girls that were raped and sexually violated as adolescents whom became single parents of kids by unknown or unfit fathers were not only forced to become mothers, but due to them being robbed of an education, they really didn't have much to pass on to their daughters so that they could have better prepared their born or the up and coming generation of daughters.

As the family increased, fathers were compelled to work long hours. They didn't had a choice, because without an education to get better paying jobs in a market where their skin color was the leading requirement for consideration; and by their current jobs paying just enough to get by; with growing families their commitment was to their employer, no matter the extensive hours separated from their sons.

That dedication and those long hours kept them away from their families, which restricted them from being strong fathers to their sons to really teach them how to be good qualified respectable men despite the picture that was painted of them by those of the other race.

This trend recycled itself into the next generation and the next generation. As the generations passed on, the number of uneducated teen mothers grew with not much more than what they had received themselves when they were teen parents. As babies continued to give birth to babies, leaving them alone to parent themselves in environments that were violent, perverted and cruel; the act became a routine of slack acceptability and developed communities of teen parents.

Today as we now journey through this Twenty-First Century generation, most live their lives in fear as a result of the little that was issued due to disadvantage. This is a disadvantaged generation whom night after night go from awful homes to terrible streets to dreadful schools; all in violent envious hate infested neighborhoods and back again; the work of those whom felt the need to deprive a generation of parents of good qualified traits, opportunities, and education.

I must admit; there are youths that have lost their way and prefer to keep it that way, continuously pointing the finger at everyone else for their lack of direction and inappropriate behavior, simply because it is easier to blame than it is to take responsibility for their action. They are the ones that the law should and must throw the book at whenever they violate regulations.

However, there are those who are just disadvantage due to poverty and lack of support. They don't like the way they live or the environment that houses them and do all that they can respectfully to live better lives; but it is just too hard for them to remain productive and proactive when it seem the world had abandon them as a result of where and what they call home.

In America, the Bahamas and a few other countries one of the main causes for many of our teens being in the streets getting themselves involved in criminal behavior is as a result of most of their parents aren't much older than they are; a lot are uneducated high school dropouts, many work long hours at low paying jobs due to being burdened down with a number of children, and the vast majority is left alone to parent themselves and each other as young as five and six.

This, as a result, gives the media room to splendidly parent neglected kids of these nations, and they not only lure them to a life of crime, but also keep the country in fear by what is most often reported. The media and the philosophy of the world with its rebellious nature taught them that using violence as a form of retaliation to problem solving is acceptable and the answer to disputes.

They constantly live their lives on a consistent alarming edge; alerted at all time, prepared, willing and able to attack if the slightest thought of threat whistles through their minds. Because of that, the average person don't think, especially teenagers; they simply react; most often through violence.

Statistics shows that 65% of teens that had committed violent acts were exposed to domestic violence or were physically abused themselves. Unfortunately; these teens lashes out in violence as a result of past experiences and to defend what they value.

Allow me to give you some history of where our country came from and what it is rapidly racing toward as it relates to rejected abandoned children, intolerant practices and discrimination against sexual gender and preferences.

From nineteen ninety five to two thousand seven there were more than fifty school shootings in America alone by shooters between the age of six (6) and thirty (30). This number doesn't include those that have hurt and killed others domestically outside of incidents involving schools. Those numbers rang between four (4) and twenty-two (22).

I want you to pay close attention to a number of important factors; the very first factor I want you to pay attention to is the age of these shooters and how they had lost their lives even before they really had begun to live them. Consistently, year after year; shooting after shooting followed each other as the number of victims escalated from two to fourteen.

One life lost is far too many, and you would think giving these stunning statistics of shootings regarding our youths, which resulted in lives lost, others would think twice before targeting another innocent victim to bully or haze. But, it seems like the greater the number of victims, the greater the motivation and behavioral pattern to continue.

In May of 2005 two teenage boys allegedly beat and kicked a homeless man to death. When asked why they did it, they said, "We were bored and wanted to have some fun, so that was what we did for fun".

I beg you please, don't be shock, because this kind of behavior occurs all the time; not only in America, but throughout the world, and I'm beginning to think that life has no value anymore even to children. We have adjusted ourselves to violence that even children can go out and take another person's life, all in the name of "Fun".

October 14, 2005 four young men intentional and brutally slaughtered a nineteen year old male at a popular night club in Nassau, Bahamas. I unfortunately knew one of the perpetrators whom participated in the beating and stabbing death of that young man as a result of a professional working relationship.

It broke my heart to face the thought of this young man having to spend the rest of his life behind the walls of a violent prison system, because he seemed to be a very nice person when we were co-workers; nonetheless, it devastated me even more when I read how he and three other friends beat and stabbed that young boy even after he had fell to the floor lifeless over a dispute regarding a female whom may have slept with all of them and probably wasn't really interested in any.

Although I didn't personally know him or any member of his immediate family, today I extend my love and words of encouragement to the Fulford family.

Between July eighth and July twenty-third of two thousand and seven, nine young persons were murdered on the streets of the Commonwealth of the Bahamas in respective incidents. Four of which were teens and most of the perpetrators responsible for their murders was also teenagers ranging from ages thirteen to twenty years of age.

Recently a young boy was pulled of his school bus and beaten almost lifeless by those of the same school. But, this comes as no surprise, because we have seen these kinds of attacks almost as much as we've heard our national anthem sang in our schools.

This type of behavior forces victims to resort to drastic measures such as murder/suicide to rid themselves of violent abusive attacks. However, the law seems to drag its feet when it comes to prosecuting perpetrators to the full extent of the books.

These are barbaric acts that are raining our nation down into the gutter. Yes, I'm talking about our country, the place we all call home; which has transformed to, but a mere shadow of its quaint, colonial form; having now been characterized by senseless acts of violence, derange, demented behavior, all because our own families, neighbors and friends have forgotten about what a true nation is all about and begin targeting, beating, abusing, and murdering each other; destroying homes across the world's foundation.

Our beautiful country and homes are floating on rivers of innocent blood of black mothers and children; rivers of blood of our innocent soldiers that were forced to go to fight unnecessarily; and rivers of innocent blood of our children fighting in the streets and being slaughtered through gang violence.

Thousands of lives are slaughtered every year for the purposes of freedom and equality. Yet, this country still isn't free, truthfully speaking. We travel hundreds of thousands of miles to defend our country from terrorists and murderers when they are living, breathing and lurking in our own backyards, homes, and neighborhoods.

We keep ourselves alerted and aware of those with ugly faces, long beards, long gammons and bad accents, while we overlook the young and attractive, whom dress themselves in expensive suits and speak using the best choices of words with PhD's behind their names; not realizing that they are those whom are raping and violating our children's innocence, holding hostage our churches, schools and robbing our youths of their worth and value, their character, their self-esteem, their youth, their lives and their freedom to be whomever they desire and love whoever they wish.

I guest, if this is the price of "Freedom", then allow me to continue to be a slave to the days and teachings of old, where families got together and discuss their problems with one another, ending conflicts with handshakes and apologies. Let me live in a world where gays, lesbians and transgenders aren't being targeted, beaten and bashed with words as a result of who they are. Allow me to live in the days when we shared our plate with the poor, which will be enough freedom for me.

Our children once walked hand in hand to schools without fear and trembling of those lurking on passage ways or those waiting at school to hurt or bully them. The fraise "I'm going to kill you" is more often use these days than words "I love you".

They push each other away and don't hesitate to use violence against them nowadays rather than embracing, welcoming, and exercising the attitude of brotherly love toward others.

We must first rid our school halls, street corners, churches, and work places of these gold plated domestic terrorists before we can cross international waters to fight crimes, because, it makes absolutely no difference between long bearded men taking over airplanes to crash into buildings killing thousands, and misguided students taking schools hostage to kill as many of our children as they can, before turning the gun on themselves.

We must understand that a life is a life, and one life is too much to lose. Violence is not an STD decease that travels through the bloodstream of a mother, transferring to a child during pregnancy. However, it is a barbarian behavior that is observed, provoked, developed and triggered from acts transpiring in the home, school, and or on our streets among families, neighbors, and residential individuals.

Teens carry around an abundance of stressful thoughts, hurt and pain depending on the magnitude of what takes place in their environment, in addition to the anger of just being teens and having to deal with day to day situations such as peer pressure, poverty, family issues, and other related conflicts are youths with unchained thoughts and are ticking time bombs.

There is only so much one can take, whether they are adults or children. Having to repeatedly deal with victimization and intolerant attacks is like being behind the prison walls where desperation compels you to sell the identity of your own mother to get out from behind enemy lines.

I'm a victim of violence, hazing, bullying and teasing; therefore, I can personally say that it pushes you to that edge that you almost are willing to do whatever it takes to have it stop, even if that means hurting the individual or individuals who is inflicting it upon you.

People seem to always complain about school shootings and say they are desperately seeking answers to what causes or drive children to kill. But the truth is, when you are caught inside the madness of intolerance, bullying and fun making, it is like being in the center of a hurricane and no one really realizes the destruction until the damage is already done. It is not always planned or wanted; simply provoked.

However, nothing just happens, and someone always knows something of what goes on in the life of a hurting child. Nevertheless; for the sake of "I don't want to get involve" and "It is not happening to me", they ignore the abuse and put a deft ear to victim's desperate cries of help.

Most of these teenage shooters put up with years of abuse and harassment by other fellow students. It may have started off at first as a joke, but as it continued and others got involved, it was no longer funny; at least not for the victims. By the time the abuse had stopped, neither victim nor perpetrator was laughing and it was too late to say I'm sorry.

If one, only one had only taken the courage to stop it when it is sparking, it wouldn't give room to flame and there would be a decrease in victims of violent attacks, a decrease in suicides, a decrease in substance abuse, and a decrease in teen pregnancy. Believe it or not, but most of what we ask our children to endure, a lot of the adults wouldn't put up with.

Being victimized and having your advantage repeatedly taken is nothing to joke about, and it's so much easier to ask a victim to turn the other cheek when the cheek that is being slapped isn't yours. Yet, this is done to innocent children who already have enough problems growing up into this cruel sadistic sinful world.

The should be concerning themselves with trying to get a good education so that they can get quality paying jobs to at least keep their heads above water in these troubling times as future parents and family providers. Certainly, they don't need the added aggravation of harassment, bullying, bodily harm, and possibly death.

I'm sure parents of high school dropouts and those that had completed, dropped out and graduated without much more than when they had entered the institution, and maybe that is because they are fighting for their lives and freedom all day from bullies and insecure giant personalities at the schools, which don't leave them much room to get an education.

Intolerant practices need to cease. What a difference it would be if only one person would stand up and speak against it and challenge these perpetrators when it is being executed.

Take a stand so that it won't continue to house itself behind the walls of our schools, on our streets and in our society. We say "What can I do, for I'm only one person". But, we should never underestimate the power of one, because if one life is saved by you picking up that single starfish out of many and throwing it back into the water, you have done more than enough. However, if you walk on by and continue to allow this behavior to continue, then a bay of starfishes on the seashore will not only punish and die, but you will also defeat your purpose for living.

IF I ONLY KNEW!
THE WORDS WE DIDN'T GET
TO SAY.

I've trusted many that failed and left me to weep,
I've drunk from the cup of disappointment, and pain beyond skin deep.
I've dreamt many dreams, some I still can not explain,
The endless devotion of unselfishness; sacrifice through fire and rain.
I was patient and forgiving, when others were forsaken,
Yet, I kept on pursuing, even at times when I was self destructing.
 If I only knew it was going to be your last walk out that door,
I would have said I love you and give you a kiss, yet once more.
Though you've caused me pain, I should've never allowed it to sink in,
But, I thought; surely there is tomorrow to forgive the anger, and from my cup
you drink.

I failed, faltered, and continue to condemn,
Even days after I saw you, again and again.
It never came to me, until the day you died,
The table had turned, now it is my time to cry.
Love continues to forgive, it defies all explanation,
It glows in all its beauty, a secret like the mysterious creation.

I thought I would get another chance to forgive and help you, but I was
wrong,
My pain continues to deepen, reflecting on how violently you had gone.
Though for the life you lead, it was destined to be,
It was a self painted picture, after friends, family and now myself, all forsaken
thee.
Eric, Dillon and Conrad Clarke, may God forgive and accept thee,
Though we don't deserve it, may your hearts forgive those that harm you; this
includes me.

INTOLERANT ATTACKS & CONSEQUENCES

Intolerant practices seem to be the norm at many of our schools. It is still going strong even after horrific shootings and depressing suicides. These practices are displayed even in the presence of teachers and administrators; yet they do nothing or not enough to stop and prevent it from continuing.

The cause of violence in our schools is primarily intolerance of anyone who is different from what society dictates and depict as normal. Students victimize others as a result of inferiority. "Empty cans make the most noise" and in order for them to feel superior, they bully others to get the attention and recondition they crave.

The media has also taught them that poverty, respectful characteristics and virtue is the thing of the past. Nowadays, poverty display a sign of curst to others. It is disrespected and refuted by those whom laugh at less fortunate others. They are teased, hazed and bullied due to this sign of considerable weakness.

They are constantly targeted for fun making, and it seems as though the system that was put in place to supposedly protect them, is failing to execute its duties and instead, focuses on the beauty of how things look from the outside rather than solving the problem.

Kids have a lot of anger, this is why they hurt others. Anger is a primary emotion that will be exposed by teens that are unable to express themselves, the hurt and pain they were forced to consume in their day to day lives and the thought of feeling weak and defeated as a result of hidden secrets, especially teenage boys.

When anger occurs, the body goes instantly into a series of mind-body reactions involving hormones, the nervous system and the muscles. This involves a release of adrenaline, which results in shortness of breath, skin flushing, muscle rigidity, and tightening in the jaw, stomach, shoulders and hands.

All of us have different events that can trigger anger. But, in most cases the event is something that serves to make us feel threatened. It is our interpretation of the event that often sends us instantaneously into an angry rage, and if the event taps into our unsolved issues regarding rejection, humiliation, being controlled and or abused, we are likely to interpret it as a threat; therefore, we react.

If we rely on rigid patterns of thinking, then we are more likely to justify our anger. A common myth suggests that healthy happy people don't get angry. But nothing can be further from the truth. How often have we been told never to show our anger, never to express it, to be a man and never to cry?

Indeed; for those who are unfamiliar with anger, the likelihood of it catapulting into rage becomes a real possibility. When things are at its most extreme, people can get hurt, damaging words are often said, and properties usually get destroyed.

How many persons, especially males were made to feel ashamed for expressing their anger, only to turn their anger inward and be chastised for feeling this very normal emotion.

The way we handle anger in adulthood has much to with the strategies we have learned in our earlier years as well as the role model we were exposed to. This is different with teens that are growing up in an age of peer pressure, hungriness for acceptance, and mix messages fed to them through modern technology.

Some may feel as though venting anger will dissipate it. However, research argues against this myth. Venting anger unproductively usually increases the probability of aggressiveness. When anger gets out of control, the consequences can be devastating and irreparable.

When people, especially teens get at that destructive level, usually a series of steps should be taken to avoid violent interaction. Their quickness to rush to physical reaction to anger with a rush of adrenaline causes stress, quick movements, fragmented thoughts, and miscommunication.

They go into an automatic showcase of negative thoughts, which increases fearful thinking and perception of being harmed and will justify their physical reaction reasoning. These views usually involve self-righteous beliefs and desire for vengeance.

There is often little logic associated with these feelings; they engage in name-calling, threats to the other person, self-justification, and assumptions that their lives are being threatened and in endangerment.

Examining anger often mean taking a journey into our past; into our inner lives and shoveling buried secrets and emotions that we wish not to face. Our anger is a mirror of injustices that have been committed against us in earlier years. It reflects our fears of vulnerability, our rejections, and our invalidations.

Coming to terms with our anger also mains resolving historic issues, letting go, forgiving responsible perpetrators and then facing life anew with flexibility, compassion and true integrity.

When people are in rage they often want to overwhelm their opponent or individually responsible persons whom contributed or fueled that angry emotion. However; they fail to understand the fact that consequences of a burning rage can generally backfire, influence harm and introduce death.

Uncontrollable rage results in respectable persons losing credibility, self respect, model characteristics, regrettable consequences and legal action following damages caused by heated temper, in addition to a lost of freedom.

I wish persons, especially children killers had not resorted to such heinous brutal methods and for those whom lived to share their reasons their actions; thought it was and is necessary for them to be punish, building more prisons to house them is like building more hospitals and morgues to accommodate sick and dying bodies that are pouring into them in great numbers, rather than trying to seek solutions to sickening deadly symptoms.

There is too many of our children falling victims to the streets as it relates to violence and we shouldn't allow them to just kill out each other and build morgues to house their bodies, but implement programs that would help to save their lives and expand their intellect as it relates to consequences of their actions.

Prison serves as a temporary restraint for prisoners and for first time offenders interacting with actual hardcore coldhearted criminals; it in return, dehumanizes them by reason of survival and having a voice. At the beginning of what is experienced in prison one becomes disturbed by the violence; at second glance they are bothered, but before they complete a fraction of their first year sentence, a body lying on the floor fatally stabbed will be just another dead body to walk by.

Teenage first time offenders have to react in violence as seasoned convicts do almost daily to stand against the giants they live and breathe among; it is like sending a tame wolf back into a pack of wild wolves. That decision can be fatal. Either that broken wounded wolf react and hunt like the others, or it would be killed. One way or the other, violence is going to be introduced to the pack.

In others cases you'll find teenagers turning to suicide as a way of overcoming mental and emotional pains, teasing, intolerance, hazing and victimization, which I have repeatedly said is not the answer to solving or ridding ourselves of any problem there may be.

On the 26th April, 2005 a friend of mine from the islands of Trinidad & Tobago sent me an email informing that his 17-year-old male schoolmate had jumped off the building of their university taking his own life. He went on to say that the young man was a very intelligent student whom had everything going for him, being on the top of his class academically. But, he said the young man had no friends and the one girl he at times hung out with were the girlfriend of one who mistreated him.

He said before the kid took his life he was bullied a lot and as a result, he hid himself into his dormitory room, away from everyone else to rid himself of the abuse, which he often did to escape sufferings and fun making.

My heart became weakened with sorrow and sadness when I read this. I felt as though I was in that kid's shoe and I wished I was in his environment during his life to appreciate his value on earth, because our lives is extremely important, precious and essential to this world; this is why we were put here on earth, and we equally deserve to live comfortable lives.

Folks, we may never know the reason behind that kid's suicide; neither will we know why teens in general commit murder, suicide or both. Just recently an eleven-year-old boy by the name of Jaheem Herrera sadly hung himself in his closet as a result of name-calling and gay slurs. Today I wish to extend my heartfelt sympathy and love to little Jaheem's parents and family.

But; in light of Jaheem's tragic passing, for the sake of future Jaheem Harreras, I'm going to share that little boy's last day of life, which today, was his most important. I will also identify key points and express his feelings on that day to those with unanswered questions of why in the prime of his youth, little Jaheem, filled with joy and brilliance, took his life (courtesy of CNN reporting, Atlanta, GA.).

"Eleven-year-old Jaheem Herrera woke up on April 16, 2009 acting strangely. He wasn't hungry and he didn't want to go to school. But, the outgoing fifth grader packed his bag and went to school at Dunaire Elementary School in DeKalb County, Georgia.

He came home much happier than when he left in the morning; smiling as he handed his mother Masika Bermudez a glowing report card full of A's and B's. She gave him a high-five and he went upstairs to his room as she prepared dinner.

A little later, when his younger sister called him to come down to eat, Jaheem didn't answer. So, mother and daughter climbed the stairs to Jaheem's room and opened the door. They found him hanging by his belt in the closet.

"I always use to see these things on TV, dead people on the news," says Bermudez. "I saw somebody die and to see this dead person is your son, hanging there, a young boy. ... to hang yourself like that, you've got to really be tired of something."

Bermudez said bullies at school pushed Jaheem over the edge. He complained about being called gay, ugly and "The virgin" because he was from the Virgin Islands. "He use to say Mom they keep telling me this ... this gay word, this gay, gay, gay. I'm tired of hearing it, they're telling me the same thing over and over," she told CNN, as she wiped away tears from her face.

But, while she says her son complained about the bullying, she had no idea how bad it had gotten. "He told me, but he just got to the point where he didn't want me to get involved anymore, because nothing was done," she said.

Bermudez said she complained to the school about bullying seven or eight times, but it wasn't enough to save him. "It apparently got worst and worst and worst until Thursday," "Just to walk up to that room and see your baby hanging there. . ."

She said Jaheem was a shy boy just trying to get a good education and make friends. "He was a nice little boy," Bermudez said through her tears. "He loved to dance. He loved to have fun. He loved to make friends. And all he made at school were enemies."

Bermudez said she thinks her son felt like nobody wanted to help him; that nobody stood up and stopped the bullies. Maybe he said you know what; I'm tired of telling my mom, she's been trying so hard, but nobody wants to help me.

Trying desperately to understand what went wrong, Bermudez asked her son's best friend to recount what happened on the day Jaheem killed himself. He said "He was tired of complaining, tired of these guys messing with him," Bermudez said, recalling the conversation with Jaheem's best friend. "Tired of talking, I think to his teachers, counselors and nobody is doing anything, **"The best way out is death**."

"The best way out is death". Wow, what such heart piercing words to read from the lips of a baby based on what was observed and recorded on the pages of his mind after his best friend committed suicide. Words like that frighten me, because although I want the existing problem to cease, I don't want to create or rather continue this cycle of suicide among our babies.

Little Jaheem Herrera felt abandoned. He felt weak. He felt deceived and that his trust and friendship was manipulated and taken advantage of. He felt scorn, diseased, and plagued as a result of the gay slurs that school and class-mates portrayed dirty, nasty and beat his spirit down with.

On the morning of April 16ᵗʰ Jaheem got up broken, this is what seem to be a "Strangely" behavior to his mother that morning. He didn't felt like go-ing to school that morning. But, he couldn't tell his mother that, because if he had, she would have questioned it, which probably would have resulted in her going back to the school's administrators, and according to him, escalated the painful slurs, bashings and name-callings; which he didn't wanted.

Therefore; with love and hope in his heart for a better day, he packed his bag and head out to school. However, by the time of the mid-day hour, eleven-year-old Jaheem knew that day would be his last. He made up into his mind to end his life before the long hand of the clocked had clicked to its final minute to close the school day.

His best friend, the kid whom was asked to retrace his steps retraced the obvious. He retraced what he recorded on the slabs of his own memory from observing the abuse of his friend. However, he was unable to retrace Jaheem's conclusion.

I guest, based on that day's strange-like behavior, the best friend might have felt Jaheem may have discovered some sort of comforting solution to his problem and rather than being depressed all the time, he found ways to laugh through it all. Certainly I'm sure, he couldn't have imagined that day would be the last and that his friend would take his life only hours later.

Little Jaheem concluded that very day would be the last of the abuse, and since it seem as though everyone had abandoned him or wasn't doing enough to help rid him from the problem, he decided to helped himself the best way an eleven year old knew without having to cause too much uproar. Sadly it was suicide, which I'll once again say is not the way to go.

Jaheem underscored many important points throughout that day, but it is one particular point I want to highlight. This point brings me back to when I said that day was the most important. It was his most important; because it was the day he demonstrated to the world the fact that he had purpose for living and took his education serious. He wanted to live and his life was worth living, and if not for his abusers who manipulated him into thinking other-wise, he would today be on this earth.

Madam Bermudez; personally I did not know your son. However, ac-cording to the history of your son's life and the step you and he both took in attempt to relieve him from the attacks that was daily administered, in addition to being a victim of a variety of abuse myself, I want to say that the faces of victims change, but abuse is the same.

Your son doesn't hold you responsible for his tragic decision on April 16th, 2009. He really doesn't. However, that day was difficult for those he loved and those who loved him as it was for him personally to have pretended to be happy when he certainly wasn't. But, he knew if he had expressed the "Normal" behavior as before and had again opened up to you about the level of suffering he was enduring at school, you may have acted out on it and the following day would have gotten worst having had to walk and breathe among future monsters he spent six hours five days a week with.

Little Jaheem truly felt in his heart that he was releasing his mother from all the burden he thought he was putting on her as a result of his constant complaints of bullying and teasing. He thought it would be best and easier on everyone if he had taken himself out of the picture, because it seemed no one could help him, and those whom could have; refused to. Unfortunately, he did just that.

It hurts me when a child as young as Jaheem have to turn to suicide to rid himself from intolerance because of feeling abandoned and neglected in an environment that suppose to protect him. It really do and I'm beginning to think we have become so accustom to these kinds of things that we simply allow life to go on intentionally forgetting the history of previous attacks, while ignoring signs to prevent future occurrences.

I can still hear the voice of little Jaheem Herrera and many others crying out from the grave on behalf of future victims and other innocent blood of our babies that have painted the walls of our schools in a rich bold red painful color. That reason alone should encourage us to unearth a no tolerance for intolerance and do whatever it takes necessarily to rid our schools of these rebellious aggressors.

Personally; I think the first step President Obama and the rest of the governing party should do is to start with writing back into law prayer into the schools, because without God's leadership and protection, this present generation with its vulnerably idle hands is Satan's team of helpers to destruct the quality and fundamentals of our forefathers.

When our children lashes out, retaliating in horrific violence we put our faces in the palm of our hands and cry out to God for answers, pleading to Him to protect our children and to give us the opportunity to prevent others.

Yet, when a child cries out for desperate help from bullies, hazing and teasing we angrily demand that they "Tough up, be a man and not a sissy" and send them back onto the battlefield. That is like wanting a fire to stop consuming our proud possessions, but rather than extinguishing it with water, we douse it with gasoline.

Only little Jaheem Herrera, others like him and youths that had killed knew what they were going through suffering at the hands of those who intentionally humiliated them by horrible means time and time again, and after being victimized, abused and used as sexual toys for perpetrators, having their cries go to deft ears, and their tears ignored; they took control of the wheel and did what they thought was best for themselves at that point, which doesn't make them killers or fools for killing and turning to suicide, though they had killed. It simply makes them desperate victims.

I won't judge them as a result, because rather than us pointing the finger at desperate victims, we should point the finger at ourselves for observing the abuse and not having the manhood to stand up for them against the giants who inflicted repeated abuse, name-calling and fun making. Don't just take the word of school administrators if the child continues to complain. Continue to push and beat down doors until you get some satisfactory results. After all, it's either that or you burying your child.

The signs are visible in the life of children that is suffering from depression as a result of abuse and intolerant practices. So visible, that it paints a complete picture to us, blessing us with vast opportunities to help prevent, not only internal trials and tribulations, but external problems as well, which is the greatest gift one can ever give.

Parents seem to lose faith in their children nowadays; they take pride in talking down to them and are too busy to take time out with their children to developed that bone of trust whereas they can know when their children are hurting and going through sufferings.

It is important for them to invest quality time into their children to develop and maintain a good relationship so that they would know how their day went at school and in their daily lives or if they are struggling with problems, future goals or suffering from depression.

Let us prevent ourselves from separating and singling out others because of race, wealth, creed, sexual gender and preferences, and nationalities. We must develop a no tolerance for intolerance in our schools, on our streets, in our environments, and start investing our time making ourselves visible in the lives of the future of this world, lending our shoulders to them to cry on, our hands of help, and a pair of ears to listen to their problems, instead of pretending to be too busy for them.

We listen to countless stories of those in regret as they observed abuse, beatings, rapes and murder of others. Yet, we fail to take action against perpetrators. "If only someone had done something to help, maybe it might have prevented the tragedy". This is often said. However, don't stand and watch a problem occur and walked away because it wasn't your problem, and then cry out in regret later. After all, what if or I should have done something would have no meaning due to almost and shoulda woulda coulda not counting.

"People should matter more than profits" and we must "Be the change we want to see in the world". Allow the person you are waiting for to lend a helping hand, a voice and a shoulder to be the very same person looking back at you in the mirror with names, "You & Me.

DEAR MOTHERS!

When I recall the memory of yesterday, the bitter words, the storm, the strife,
I thank our Lord for you, again and again today, because to me, you gave the gift of life.
Heart filled with darkness, mind empty and meaningless, because of that, I gave failure, pain and court cases.
Heightened feelings, rejection to the love you tried to give,
The way I learned, was the way I lived.
The day I held, was a day I feared,
The morning I discovered my mother dead.

Dear mother, if I had one more yesterday,
I would be your child again; humble, respectful, loving in every way.
Dear mother, if I had one more star to wish upon,
I would wish for no other, because you were my number one.
Mother, if I had just one more prayer to pray,
I would ask God to take me, and allow you to stay.

Sometimes I was not aware of things,
The words you spoke, the decisions made, or the melodies you sing.
Yet, I lived my life not caring at all,
Not seeing the beauty of your love, both great and small.
Suddenly that morning, I awoke to find,
That reality; my mother gave her life to save mine.

Renewed once more, I'm aware,
Your love for me, it expresses itself, both far and near.
These words were spoken to me, from your heart's throne,
Beckon child, please come on home.
Thank you mother for your happiness,
But, most of all, your love and forgiveness.

THE SEPTEMBER 11TH
COLUMBINE MESSAGE

On October 22nd, 2002 Oriana Fallaci addressed an audience at the American Enterprise Institute. Ms. Fallaci, a native of Florence, Italy and a life-long journalist caused turmoil across Europe with the publication of her book, "The Rage and the Pride".

She Writes "Since September 11th we are at war, because the frontline of that war is here in America. When I was a war correspondent, I liked to be on the frontline, but this time, in this war, I do not feel as a war correspondent, I feel as though I'm a soldier.

The duty of a soldier is to fight, and to fight this war I deploy a personal weapon. It is not a gun; it's a small book, The Rage and The Pride. My soldier's weapon is the weapon of truth. The truth that begins with the truth I maintain in these pages.

From Afghanistan to Sudan, from Palestine to Pakistan, from Malaysia to Iran, from Egypt to Iraq, from Algeria to Senegal, from Syria to Kenya, from Libya to Chad, from Lebanon to Morocco, from Indonesia to Yemen, from Saudi Arabia to Somalia; the hate for the West swells like a fire fed by the wind, and the followers of Islamic fundamentalism multiply like a protozoa of a cell which splits to become two cells then four then eight then sixteen then thirty-two to infinity.

Those who are not aware of it only have to look at the images that the television brings to us every day. The clash between us and them is not a military clash. Oh no; it is a cultural one, a religious one, and our military victories do not solve the offensive of Islamic terrorism. On the contrary, they encourage it, they exacerbate it, they multiply it, and the worst is still to come".

President Bush has said "We refuse to live in fear." That's a beautiful sentence, very beautiful, I loved it. But, it is inexact Mr. President, because the West does live in fear.

I accuse us also of a crime; it is the loss of passion. Haven't you understood what drives our enemies? What permits them to fight this war against us? They have passion, so much passion that they die for it".

I want you to pay special attention as she talks about the frontline of the war being here in America, our beloved country and called herself a "Soldier" in the front line of that war. But, rather than her carrying nine millimeters and knives, her weapon is a book of knowledge to educate the people that the real war is not the war we're spending billions of dollars funding every year, even though that war of safety is important.

She warns that the war is the war among ourselves and our own people, and unless we become a nation of one again, we're fighting a losing battle.

Politicians, lobbyists and radio pundits have all played roles in making America an exclusive country for the values of the old and not of the new. Society still frowns on race, creed, interracial relationships, and gives hostility towards homosexuals and transgender persons.

I wonder when America will become the country where her children do not see differences and will actual fight the war in her own land before the one which many of her offspring are sacrificed abroad.

"A society that is calling for the end of slavery and brutality are slaves themselves". This country is founded by the people, yet controlled by the few, the powerful, and the rich. We work to live; we are slaves to bosses, slaves to our government heads, slaves to money, and slaves to ignorance.

Paper with numbers of value is defined as survival, power, self worth, and develops fame. We work forty plus hours a week just to eat and to have a place to live; the rest is used on luxury material to feed self satisfaction.

How many people in this country are truly happy?

We deceive ourselves in believing that wealth brings happiness, this is why there are many, especially teens who are motivated by having lots of money. This hunger feeds desperate desires, which allows them to go to great degrading levels to get it and maintain wealth. They believe that once they become in arms reach of great wealth it will then open up that door to happiness. This can't be more further from the truth.

Fathers are separating themselves from their family and sons and committing their time to the workplace as a result fear of returning back to the poverty that is written on the pages of their life's history. They were traumatized as youths and what they went through having to go without or due to the harsh experience of poverty, they fight to give what was missing in their past to their children and families.

How many are truly miserable?

The rich look down upon the poor and expect them to be miserable and unhappy as a result of poverty. Although it is frustrating when a mother is unable to feed her babies, and despite the fact that poor folks hate the thought of being poor when it is highlighted by those whom are fortunate enough to advertise that myth of life not having worth unless one live above and beyond their means; poor folks lead the greatest lives, because though they are disadvantaged to opportunities, they live their lives true to who they are and in freedom.

How long must we be slaves?

A friend of mine in Atlanta, Georgia, Unite States once asked me after overhearing a conversation I had with a member of customer service in the office of the United States Internal Revenue Service (IRS) a few months back when I was at that point preparing a life and career in America.

From the outside of our phone conversation he heard me say to the pleasant customer service personnel that I did not wished to become an American citizen, but simply wanted a way where I could have paid taxes equally to the natives if I was going to stay and embark on a career in the country and receive revenue.

After closing on the conversation with the government agent he asked why I didn't want to become a citizen of the United States; a country that is rich and "Free". Without hesitation, I told him although I'm a lover of his country and thanks to his President Barrack Obama and his boldness that had inspired me, I won't apply to become a citizen of America, because I do believe that my country, the Bahamas is crying out for a leader at a time like this to lead this modern generation through the twenty-first century and I want to run for that office the way Mr. Obama did. However, based on the word "Free", I didn't stop there.

With respects to his country and who I am as an experienced person, I told him I'm free without being a citizen of America, because slavery is in the mind and unless Americans, the people of the Bahamas and other blind-eyed nations free their minds from the fraise freedom and understand what freedom is, I'm sorry to disappoint them, but the country is a slave to its ignorant thoughts.

Put on your thinking caps and look outside the box of your own reality and try to understand what I'm saying. If we, the people knew what freedom was all about, honestly; a military officer wouldn't be called to fight for his nation, but asked to keep their sexuality a secret, in fear of attacks and supposed friendly fire.

If this country was really free, the flag of color; rather than being flown at half-staff, it would be brought down and accepted widespread as it relates to inter-racial dating, equality, fairness and opportunity.

If this country was really free, innocent persons like Mr. Luis Ramirez and homeless citizens sleeping on the streets of America will not be targeted and beaten almost lifeless and later died just because violent groups felt the need to target them for being disadvantaged and of another race.

If this country was actually free, gays, lesbians, bisexuals and transgender persons will not be treated as outcasts and have churches and other organizations close their doors to them as a result of who their hearts chose to love.

If this country was actually free, students like C. J. Bills and Tim Dahl from Franklin Sr. High School will not be pelt and discriminated against because of their sexuality.

If this country was actually free persons like Matthew Sherpard, Sean Kennedy, Teena Brandon, Lawrence King, and others would not be in their graves today; beaten and murdered because they were homosexuals.

If this country was free, hate crimes, gay and racial slurs and fear would be a thing of the past and not to the frontline governing with such a barbaric fist that it compels eleven-year-olds like little Jaheem Herrera and others to choose death over life, taking their own lives in hope of getting comforted.

If this country was free sick persons wouldn't have a chance to die on hospital beds where they suffered and fought for healthcare, eventually dying from a double battle lost to deceases and insurance companies. Genuine freedom would provide them with an opportunity of treatment, because persons would care a lot more about people than profits.

Finally; if this was a genuinely free nation, God, the Creator of Heaven and Earth would not have to bring a nation to its knees in order to elevate a black educated highly qualified gentleman to the office of the presidency.

I guest what I'm saying is, take the fraise of freedom out from your minds and focus on ideas that defeat capitalism, which have been branded tyrannical and incompetent with a growing society. Yet, we wonder why depression grows in an alarming rate and crime has mounted over our heads. Money is the sword of the twenty-first century in which decides the fate of a society.

Will an idea finally diminish the blade or will society continues to frown on differences and be controlled? Should we allow the lives of the many men and women who fought for us over the years and continues to fight every day of their lives to go in vain or without purpose?

September 11th, 2001 the world was on a stand still as they watched two 747 airliners carrying hundreds of passengers flew into the twin towers in New York City. At a lost for words I observed as some screamed desperately, a few jumped in attempt to save their lives, but rather lost it, while others ran breathlessly toward safety and the rest stood by in shock and disbelief.

Fruits bore from the act of violent hateful barbarians the day the world was forced to stop, look, and listen to the act that seem surreal. However, I saw a nation of over three hundred million people unite in love and became a nation of one. On that day they understood those terrorists was not targeting the homosexuals, but they were attacking Americans. They were not targeting the Blacks, the Hispanics, the Latinos, the Asians, or the Christians, but were in fact, attacking Americans.

They did not care about those whom had enough money to fill the Grand Canyon, or those who didn't have two pennies to rub together. They were attacking America and all those that were umbrella under its wings as citizens of this great nation.

The identities of the fatal, the broken and the wounded victims were of differences in races, sexes, and sexual orientations, gender, color and backgrounds; many of whom came from humble poverty stricken beginnings. But, on that day those whom sacrificed and gave their lives to save others were not thinking about who was gay or of a different color, but were rather thinking of those that were sheltered under the wings of the American flag; their people.

They all had one purpose, one goal, one dream in mind to accomplish and that was to give their country, this country that is united by fifty-two states a chance to make it right and allow uniformity to be a daily practicing habit so that dreams can be develop, lives can be protect, future funded, and brotherly-love kept in communities.

Reflecting back to tragedies of yesteryear, victims such as Eric Harris, his friend Dillon Klebold and others like them were bullied, pressured and taken advantage of to the point where they gave it all up and took the law into their own hands, revenging the abundance of pain, abuse and embarrassment they had endured by those they once dwell among, stemming from separation and divide.

On April 20th 1999 witnesses testified that the two young notorious gunmen walked into their school and ended the lives of twelve students and a teacher, scarring the hearts of many others, only to become victims of suicide themselves an hour later.

Pinned to my television screen at twenty two years old, I saw bodies dragged and taken from the doors and windows of that school. I saw parents running toward their children, children running toward police officers, friends hugging and holding on to foes tightly with tears draining down their faces. As a dark cloud settled over that blood-soaked environment, flowers, teddy bears and other gifts were lined off in remembrance of those that were lost.

My heart went out to them and their families. However, today I say stop the harassment and intolerant practices and there will be no need for memorials to remember our babies. We must appreciate and fight for them while they are alive, hug and kiss them and make them know that they are loved and someone is grateful to have them on earth.

Don't wait until death knocks on the doors of our hearts to regret the words we didn't say, the hugs we didn't give, the kisses we didn't kissed, the love we didn't share, the words we forgot to say, and the bravery we failed to expressed when one's advantage was taken. Celebrate their work while they are very much alive and can feel appreciated for the sacrifice, sweat and tears they had given in attempt to make this world a better place.

As I sit here writing this book, a citizen of another native land, I can still hear voices crying from the grave, because up until now, many of us whom are alive, well and fortunate to had others sacrificed and continue to give their lives fighting for our safe keeping still haven't understand the fact that the real war is internal and we must rid ourselves from these in-house barbarians before traveling to external battlegrounds to fight.

We fight against each other like animals in the wild while leaving ourselves vulnerable to the enemy who utilizes this powerful tactic to execute their destructive attacks upon us. It is thereafter that we realize our downfall to then come together as a nation of one people. Although it is good that something brought us together, we shouldn't allow the attacks of the enemy and violence being exchanged among our children to encourage us to unite and be our brothers' keeper.

The United States of America, the Bahamas, Canada and many other nations are beautiful wealthy habitations of people that can do and say most things without being harmed, killed or thrown into prison as a result. Although this is good, these environments are still in captivity and are slaves to selfish greed. We will never be completely free until these countries become societies that love and care about people.

The events of September 11th and the Columbine shootings reminded us of how important togetherness is; because "A country that is divided is a country that is headed for destruction". "United we stand, divided we fall", allow those events of yesterday to be the guiding light that will take this world into a better tomorrow.

THE UNPLANTED SEED

I remember my parents asking me as a child to wait until I had gotten older before displaying myself as an adult, which I hated because it meant that I was not able to do things I wanted to do that I thought was fun at the time. I could not wait until I had gotten older so that I could have done those things; manning my freedom and living the way I wanted to live my life.

Well; eventually I grew and got older. But, with age came responsibilities, consequences and regrets. Although I was able to do the things that interested me as an adolescent, it was no longer fun for the most part after I became an adult, because doing what I wanted can have and did came with extremely bad aftereffects.

This statement might be unknown to a few, but this is very familiar to many others, including myself. However, things just aren't the same for kids today as it relates to respectable upbringings and the way the difference of generations were and are being raised up nowadays. I have seen many of our older folks as I journey through life drop their heads in shame and disappointment as they observe the behavior of today's youths.

I know the world is changing every second of every day as modern technology globalizes the earth; because of it, our children, being birth into this technical globalization age are more vulnerable to become misguided or lured into destructive paths by a web of deception that is showcased as "Fun things". However, the old was called by God because they know the way of the world and they should never compromise their principals and standards to compete or to be a part of.

Society has twisted the language and has our youths speaking negative harsh words, while rather referring to respectable things. The word "Bitch" spoken out of the name of a young girl is today welcomed among females. "Dogg" signifies friend, and "Nigger", a word black men and boys dreaded and despised in the past is appreciated as acquaintance.

A former United States President, though I respect him for his legacy of good works, he is responsible and partially to blame for educating every ignorant teen that had access to a television the myth that engaging in oral sex; once it is done orally, it is not considered sex. In an age where Aids is dominating the youth environment, sending thousands of lives to an early grave each year, though it's a little too late and wouldn't make much of difference, I wish he would withdraw that statement.

Pornography is the new Sesame Street program for children, while methods of knifing and shooting is use to settle disputes among teenagers, instead of handshakes and apologies. Weapons and tactics that were used to keep our children on a respectable path in days of old are measures that are now prohibited, neglected and or forgotten about.

When a six year old infant can raise their hand to hit a parent or an adult, red flags should immediately go up into our minds to alert us that much more is needed than one being sent to their room with restrictions of privilege for a certain length of time.

When a fifteen year old kid could arm himself with a brass knuckle weapon and strike the face of a teacher to unconsciousness, I think it is necessary to do more than giving children detention.

When a fifteen year old can brutally murder their parents for not being allowed to see a boyfriend; that is more than enough reason for the governing party of a country to give authority to parents to do whatever it takes legally to maintain respect in the home they have to share with a child that is misguided and out of control.

Peer pressure is much more intense among our youths; choices are more abundant and extreme for them to make, and decent heroes and role models are a lot harder to find. Yet, God's word has not changed and the Bible still provides the guidelines of which we are asked to use in order to maintain a home of obedience, reverence and respect between children and parents.

The Bible has given us perfect guidelines as to how we should raise our children, and it's no doubt, clear that if we coach our children by the standards and teachings of God, when they become teenage adults those teachings will remain in their hearts and minds. As a result, good decision-making will be a lot easier to make, parents would build better relationships with their kids, and violence will decrease on our streets, in our schools, and in the home, because they will reflect on those religiously constructive seeds that were sown in their lives as children.

There are many religions out in the world, even those who are Atheist is practicing the religion of no belief. With the exception of no belief, all religion leads to god (to each its own). Well I guest even the practice of none belief still leads to a god; to none believers may surprise.

Personally; my belief is in Jesus Christ and I practice the faith of Christianity because it is a relationship between God and man. Today, I will not speak for others in respect to their faith, but for what have been proven to me, the teachings of Christ Jesus gives us dominion over all that was made and teaches us how to walk in the authority as children of those that were created.

Children must walk in the authority of their parents, guardians and even adults. It is the only way we can get a grip on violence and bloodshed. Four out of five children around the world that were brought up under the teachings of Jesus, though they may have strayed a bit, are respectable citizens of society.

Just as in every school of fishes will swim a spoil fish; in every God fearing family there is a misguided child. Nevertheless, one out of every ten children that were brought up in godly Christian homes became school bullies or committed graphic violent attacks on others, such as parent battery, domestic attacks or abusive behavior toward animals.

They understand that raping others of their lives and joy sends a direct attack on God Himself, and in the same manner of a parent being disrespected by their child or children, consequences must and should follow; action is taken against those whom harm one of His own.

It is imperative that children understand at an early age, not only the existence of God, but also His position and the authority He has given to you whom are called parents. As they learn the fact that stealing and telling tales is wrongful habits to develop, they should know they are nothing more than children who are all one in the eyes of God who made us equal, and should submit to the authority of an adult until they take on their own responsibilities.

Behind the four walls of a school's student body the force that is most important, which we must pay special attention to is called "Influence". Sooner or later, a few will become leaders when they aren't followers of others; some will take on leadership responsibilities such as class presidency and team captains, while others will lead informally as friends influencing other associates in the involvement of whatever practices they feel lead to partake in.

Today it is a lot easier for youths to follow the crowd of influence even when they know it may not be the best decision to make. But, to be a part of something and accepted by that family of peers, they will give up their morals and right to decision making to prevent that mob from turning on them.

In this modern day and time strong leaders are very rear, but they are out there among the thorns and thistles of this world. These leaders are sketchy, they are the ones who are seen as lambs, but are rather lions that will continue their pursuit until they accomplish goals set before them.

There are known leaders such as Dr. Martin L. King, Billy Graham, Bono, Michael Jackson, Sir Lynden Pinling, Sir Milo Butler, Lady Coretta Scott King, Lady Rosa Parks and others whose names have been written on the pages of history in appreciation to their hard work and dedication to making a difference in this world for the better. However, there are many unknown others whose names may never be written on history's pages and who may never receive awards, but they are also responsible for the shaping and molding of this nation.

There are teachers who know their students by names because they developed that relationship individually where they become knowledgeable of problems without it being mention.

Those religious leaders who extended and continues to extend their hearts and hands of mercy to families of hurting communities without it being broadcast to the viewing public or mentioned.

Those neighbors who opened their doors to hungry stomachs and gave shelter to those that were homeless in the name of love. And finally; those students behind the walls of our schools who refuse to bully others, bash and beat homosexuals and transgender persons with degrading slurs and physical harm, but rather expresses brotherly love and appreciation to their mates and continues to extend appreciation to those that are observed as outcasts.

All of these persons are leaders of great influence, even if only a few names are printed across billboards in lights. We must allow the influence to remain positive and maintain these practices, because after all, it is a lot easier for teens to get caught up into the frenzy of things.

We should not expect positive qualities from our children if in the home they are being taught wrongful attributes such as hatred, lawlessness, bigotry, racial and sexual discriminations, and without any form of moral or fundamentals of God.

Lack of parental guidance to a child is like taking an individual out to sea and asking them to jump overboard. Negativity surrounds us like the ocean; if our children are in environments where their brain cells is consistently bombarded with sexually explicit information of perversion and immorality, drugs, gang violence, bigotry and hate; don't expect much good to come from them.

What you will see is exactly what you will get, and I don't think we need to be rocket scientists to see what is going on around the world and in our country is as a result of misguided, neglected and abused children by parents and members of the community.

Children blindly depend on every word and rule said and given by their parents in the home even if they act like they don't, or they refuse to be govern. It is like wanting to say yes, but answering no. It is like wanting to be hugged, but as a sign of pride, they extend their hand to be shaken. And it is like wanting desperately to know and be told that they are loved and appreciated; but instead, they say you're my hommie and I gat your back.

This is the age language that we are in. However, as long as they are living in your home you must not compromise, but parent with an iron fist. Because, the same way the language has change, so did the behavior, and their way of crying out for help is taking their frustration to the streets, to our schools, and in our environments where there is a breathing ground of people just like them that will respond just like them.

God took special care in designing the role of a parent; He knew their roles were essential and no other actor would have been able to play those timely parts the way they could have. But; we must be careful.

Men must regain their places as fathers while women have to again learn how to be qualified mothers to a breathing generation. Video games are parenting our children; Satanists are parenting our children; drugs and alcohol are parenting our children; sex is parenting our children; the internet is parenting our children; the streets gives them access to more guns than the police force and it is parenting how to kill and destroy each other; pimps and madams are parenting our children; everyone and everything else is parenting our children except for parents and the bible.

Parents you are obligated and compel to do whatever it takes to keep your children in line or else their sins and condemnation will fall upon you. It is vitally important that you convince them that you will not allow their misbehavior to bring burden upon your soul. If you don't, you will have to answer for all their actions as children and if they take another person's life in their youth, their victim's blood will be upon your hands if they are under your authority, because it will mean that you haven't sown the seed you were called to sow as parents.

THE UNKNOWN ENEMY

This world; for the many centuries that it has been in existence may seem out of control as it relates to violence and other barbaric attributes; but it isn't. God, to each its own has always been and will always be in control. Yes, there are activities of crimes and evil practices that are at disturbing levels. However, it is at a controlled level, immortally speaking.

As in every bunch of apples you'll find a spoil apple that should be separated from the group; it is the same with youths and even adults who simple just want to be community hazards and resort to criminal activities for the thrill of it or because they refuse to take responsibility for their lives and wish to fault the world for their own failure.

There are others who may just want to be in control of things and everyone around them; desired not to be governed by rules, regulations and the laws of the land, which we are unable to afford them. Nonetheless, we're not going to talk about those self forbidden fruits, but will rather focus on those whom were driven to that point of no return.

Teens that had committed murder, suicide or even both; some didn't do it for reasons that is known to us, such as bullying, peer pressuring, hazing, discriminatory slurs and other methods that had triggered violence.

There are those who committed the act as a result of feeling alone, rejected, unwanted, and abandoned. Others did it out of fear, as it relates to threats of exposed secrets, fear of bodily harm stemming from constant verbal abuse, and feelings of outcast. And then, there are those who demonstrated death simply because no one cared whether they had lived or died.

Once an individual, mainly a child, concludes in their minds that death is better than life resulted from feeling unwanted, unappreciated and unloved; it will only be a matter of when, but certainly death will take its place. If revengeful, please believe they will take lives down if it's a situation where they fault others.

If it's a case of domestic abuse, you may find their parents falling victims to their violent hands. When a child lashes out, nine times out of ten, the people they display their anger toward, were not really those they intended to express it on; but innocent victims often unfortunately suffers for the fault of the guilty.

Usually; guiltless persons do sometimes be the ones caught at the bad end of the road; so to speak. Maybe the anger they had dispensed in the school halls and classrooms were fueled from behind the walls of their homes for weeks, but somehow triggered by schoolmates whom might have said or did something that may have been misinterpreted or intellectually read processed wrong, and as a result, sparked the flame which sourced the shedding of blood.

Teenagers don't only lash out on their peers; unfortunately, that anger at times is experienced by parents. Although the public rarely hears about parent battering, there are thousands, if not millions of parents that are beaten, abused, and assaulted by disorderly, misdirected, misbehaving kids on a daily base.

Like spousal abuse, parent battering is also a silent problem that's rarely discussed, and this is because most parents either blame themselves for the violence, hoping that it is an isolated incident after the first attack or they tend to hide it, refusing to accept the fact that their child or children have problems that needs to be seriously address by professionals. Instead, they construct excuses for them as a result of shame and the blueprint continues.

In other families, violence is of the norm; out of control teens beat and batter their parents in retaliation for parents attempting to display disciplinary action, restrict them from environments that may lead to destruction or persons with influence to pilot astray or seduce criminal behavior.

Whether it is physical, sexual or mental abuse by other family members, close friends of the family or parents themselves, painful conduct demonstrated on children hidden by parents has often sway parent battering.

There are a few that transpire as it relates to mental instability due to loving parents preferring to hold on to disadvantaged kids rather than releasing them to professional strangers of institutional homes, or them failing to religiously administer proper medication, which results in that instability being demonstrated on parents and other family members. But; these cases are rare.

Parents are ashamed of accepting and admitting the thought of their teens assaulting them; this is one of the reasons for the denial, while others prefer not wanting admit their inability to control and discipline their out of control kids in fear of that disciplinary action triggering that violent anger and rage that they are bearer of.

Fear is a major factor in the home. It is a proven fact that children, no matter how young posses dangerously explosive tempers. Kids had even killed adults as a result of their inability to control their anger and rage. This may be the reason why most parents, especially single mothers that are too frightened to address or approach children with any form of disciplinary action after discovering their teens' violent temper.

Although it is good and necessary to get help to kids with violent temper, that is easier said than done, parentally speaking. Only parents know the nature and capability of their children and by them seeking outside assistance from councilors or members of the police department, it may not only further damage their fractured relationship, in addition to increasing the effects of the aggression.

Apart from the foundation of the home, the law also plays a major role in their behavioral pattern. Nowadays, if a parent disciplines their kids in the slightest physical manner, such as spanking; their lives are threatened by incarceration due to laws that are in place to prohibit physical action. Because of that, there isn't really much parents can really do to maintain control in their household when dealing with disrespectful out of control teenagers who have a tendency to use the law as a crutch for parents.

I guest in the name of parenthood, the rule is to kill or be killed, because the law of the land stands hand in hand with children, giving them that backbone of support. But, who supports the right of the parent and where are the laws that say they can physically defend themselves against out of control violent teens.

Abuse is far different from disciplinary action and as an advocate for children; I totally disagree with any parent, guardian or adult violently abusing children in any shape, form or fashion.

I do feel however, there should be some form of law to prevent and protect these little angels from being abuse, but not to prevent them from being discipline. Parents should be able to use physical force to some degree to order their children when it is necessary and to avoid parent battery; after all, that is what brought the best out of many from generation to generation.

According to the instructions of God, "If you spear the rod, you'll spoil the child". This was the instructions that was executed by generations of old and has kept many of us on the straight and narrow path; compelling many to turn their lives around to become respectful members of society, and if it worked for us, it can certainly work for today's youths.

As a result of modern law that prevents parents from physically disciplining their children, I ask the question; who do we blame when children react in violence against their parents, teachers and other superiors in authority as they journey throughout this life and share the same community space as respectable citizens do?

- ↑ Do we blame them, because they should have known better than resorting to violence learnt from television?
- ↑ Do we blame their parents, because they didn't instill or maintain proper disciplinary guidelines without the usage of physical force?
- ↑ Do we blame the legislators for passing such laws preventing parents from disciplining their children physically?
- ↑ Should we hold teachers responsible, because they didn't teach them well or enough to understand the difference between respect between adults and kids?
- ↑ Or should we blame the gods, because there are so much of them and religious laws that kids become confuse and they don't know which to follow?

I'll allow you to answer that!

We as parents must question the decisions we are making for ourselves and our children. We must learn to hold our kids responsible for their actions, their words spoken and their behavioral patterns, because they are the future of our country and the takeovers of this world.

The servant should not tell their master what is needed to be done, but the master should rather dictate to the servant. Although however, our children should respectfully be given the right to live how they want to live their lives, we should be instructing and guiding them on the way they should go by doing it as long as they are under our authority.

If we don't, we'll soon come to the realization that the hallways of our schools, homes and streets won't be enough to prevent the bullets that will be flying around, while arming ourselves with swimming gears to prevent us from drowning in rivers of innocent blood.

It is clear that our teenagers are crying out desperately for help and support, but in their own way, which is not of the norm and is unfamiliar to us older folks. Nevertheless, the message is straight forward.

It is also apparent that there is a need for a lot more work to be done in order to understand why some children cope with situations and others don't. It is extremely important for us to recognize the fact that violence is a universal phenomenon on the rise and shootings conducted by kids is beginning to elevate itself to the very top of the line.

Battering and abusiveness in the home leads to children without childhood and infants without parents. Life for them then becomes a burden. Both parents and children live in constant fear and anxiety. Children experiencing abuse also have a higher risk of juvenile delinquency and substance abuse.

For every homicide victim of violence there are many survivors out there struggling with scars and mental disabilities; those whom didn't die when burnt, stabbed, shot, beaten, choked, or thrown up against the wall by perpetrators. Those who continues to attempt suicide as a result of un-acceptance, discriminatory slurs and teasing, and victimization by those refusing to live outside of the box of ignorance and stupidity.

Immediate action is always a necessity, but a holistic understanding has to be achieved to impact this cycle of silence. Parents along with the community can and should help in a number of ways, such as teaching them communication and problem solving skills, encouraging children's autonomy and independence, showing them how to handle negative thoughts and behavior, while preventing them from taking part in conflicts, victimizing, abusing and bullying others.

Parents, your role in your children's decision making is essential; only you have the script that can and will lead and guide them into paths of righteousness. However, if you're not in their lives to play your parental part, they will choose from thousands of candidates that are waiting from an auditioned pool that is willing to volunteer for your scene, and they will be cast to play your role, which suppose to make you shine.

"A copy is never as good as the original"; our central mission as parents should be to strategize crucial patterns for pointing the lives of youths in a productively positive direction. Therefore, a significant reduction of these criminal activities in our country, our schools, and on our streets should become an extreme urgency and must be addressed immediately, which not only begins in the home, but also starts once again with you and me.

LITTLE DIRT ROAD!

That little house on the hill, where mother and father lived,
And that little dirt road we used to get there; lay there still.
A steady, but gentle breeze, blowing through the trees,
And the church on the hill, that stands there still, brings back memories.

Little dirt road, do you remember me,
The little boy I use to be.
Little dirt road, I was not so tall,
Yet you carried me, barefoot and all.

No electric lights, walking through the night,
So dark at times on those windy streets, thank God for the moonlight.
Years have come and gone, I cried many tears, before going home,
I visited you my little dirt road, which lye alone.

Little dirt road do you remember when,
Little dirt road, you were my only friend.
Can you take me back, to where my parents lived?
Take me back to where they had so much to give.

Little dirt road, please take me far,
Far from these violent streets, to where we walk when there was no car.
Little dirt road, to every now and then,
Every now and then, I think of those days back when.
Little dirt road, please come take me,
Back to the church on the hill, and love in our community.

MY ENVIRONMENT

—————=ɔ●ɕ——————

"A man is judged by the company he keeps" and his life is predicated based on the environment of which he is raised up in. No matter how often the generations change, this statement has proven itself factual. Therefore, it is important to chase environments while we chase dreams.

Maybe you have forgotten or maybe you were not around to have observed; or just maybe, you were not as fortunate as others were; but our homes, street corners, neighborhood blocks, schools, work places, and our environments were once safe and tranquil surroundings. Though a few dreams were lost in translation, they were fitting to be proudly called desired places.

They were once places of peace, mercy and compassion, and if or when there were times of disagreements, it was quickly discussed and forgotten about or settled over dance competitions, apologies, smiles and handshakes. Of course this world is not perfect, so there were fights and physical exchanges, but never the bath of which we today take in blood.

People were passive and friendly; our neighborhoods were safe to the extent where one felt comfortable enough to go to bed leaving their doors unlocked without questioning the slightest thought or having fear that their homes would be burglarized by intruders lurking to kill, steal and destroy the very well being of our family's togetherness and welfare.

They were places where most were not concerned about distinguishing between suburbs of upper and lower classes, brotherly and sisterly love, and broken dreams. The essence of our neighborhoods was innocence and togetherness shared at dinner tables with those in need, not those of greed.

Innocent children once played in our streets, on playgrounds and basketball parks, where they enjoyed the warmth of innocence in being children without having to watch or worry over predators and kidnappers lurking to violate their youthful virtue through sexual attacks. Like their parents, they lived fearless.

Educational and religious institutions were places teenagers fought to attend and to be apart of its organizational bodies, because they were places of togetherness, acceptance, appreciation, respect, warmth and love. God, to each its own was the center of their message. However today, our children are more concern of whether they will become the next victim of sexual attacks like infant choir boys were, while school teachers teaches death education to students on "Suicide Day".

"There are more fears than hope" on our streets and it is a lot easier for our children to become caught up into lifestyles of criminological activities, because we have set our boundaries and teaching our babies differences between who is considered good enough to dwell among and those whom are measured as trailer trash and should be neglected and disrespected as a result of poverty and lack of opportunity.

Neighborhoods where many of us once walked hand in hand has now been separated, discarded, considerably curst from wealthy suburbs; rebirth and introduced as "The Ghetto". Families that housed in these forbidden grounds seem to also be considerably cursed by advance opportunity and welcomed to sudden destruction for they are prohibited and deemed less than human beings in the eyes of fortunate others.

Although those cursed suburbs are places the rich and famous considers being spaces of disgrace, shame and extreme hazards to wealthy families; these environments birth most of us, including presidents, doctors, professors and many other timely gifts of humble hearts and mercy.

Disturbingly; most that live in these considerably forbidden spaces feel the same way and have adapted that opinion. They have accepted and settled with mentalities of wild animals that carefully craft their signature into these streets with that rich red ink from the body of their innocent brothers and sisters, mothers and fathers, families and friends, children and babies.

Football players, rich house wives, police chiefs and others roam these territories to disclose their true identities through those they consider to be street trash; employing them to execute heinous violent attacks on their lovers and friends for a few nickel and dimes.

High profile officials strongly recommend that families in such curst environment should keep themselves armed with guns and dangerous weaponry of protection, while the media educate our children on how to use them on each other. They are the ones dumping weapons by the truck load onto those forsaken streets, yet they support their homes and properties with multi-million dollar security devices and armored guards in attempt to protect themselves from those they sold weaponry to.

Law enforcement agents confiscates illegal drugs from domestic and international traffickers for the fact that it is harmful to one's health, and they no doubt, try to prevent their children from using and abusing these deadly substances. However, they wholesale it to disadvantage vulnerable persons in these ghetto-like environments.

It seem as though children of these streets who needs help the most, are those that are most forgotten by opportunity and the focus is rather given to those of the rich and famous who don't need it.

Wealthy persons such as Miss. Oprah Winfrey grew up poor and were forsaken by most. Today however, she makes more money in a minute than most families make in a year. Yet, she often pleads to shop owners to allow her to purchase products rather than accepting handouts. Hats off to her!

Powerful white folks like Bill O'reilly take pleasure in condemning brothers like Tupac Shakur and other rap artists for using their resources, gifts and talents to help educate and elevate their people, my people; black poor people out of the ghetto and away from violence the best way they know how to connect with them. Nonetheless, his interests is not in helping ghetto folks and ceasing the shedding of blood in these environments, because if it was, he would have used his powerful platform to encourage ghetto-love rather than consistently attacking rappers who actually do something without wanting to be honored and notified.

The ghetto is a place where sexual predators embark on daily camping trips to execute their pedophilic attacks on disadvantaged vulnerable children whom are desperately awaiting opportunities to get up out of the blood washed, crime infested, hungry forbidden grounds. They use these territories as breathing grounds and set up tents, filtering into the lives of innocence, presenting themselves as sheep, but are rather wolves under clothing of sheep.

They know all to well that these grounds and those dwelling within its reach are those that are most forgotten. Therefore, police and the justice system invests less time and attention to these locations and persons that dwell in them. Because of it, they repeat their offenses, sexually assaulting again and again until justice is executed by victims themselves.

The ghetto is observed as places where low income families kill and slaughter each other cold heartedly, while those on the other side of town in upscale communities expresses brotherly love among each other, walking hand in hand. They say families in these forbidden grounds broadcasts their personal affairs onto the street, because they are those of low self-esteem, whereas those in wealthy suburbs maintain their dirty dark secrets hidden in their closets, pretending all to be well until their closets runs over compelling it to spill into their laundry rooms and eventually into the neighborhood.

Rich men creep around on their wives to run down complexes in these forbidden grounds to engage in both heterosexual and homosexual practices with men, woman and children; at times impregnating young school girls and confusing young boys of their sexuality. Yet, they are more than willing to finance abortions for their daughters who were impregnated by those they love as well as those conducted by family members and adult friends that had raped their children so that their scorn would remain in secrecy, and posts threat to homosexual lovers for being in love with their sons.

These are living acts that has built its home in those environments. Unfortunately; upon everything else that plagues children, they are force to fight practices that were brought in by those in corporate offices. However, I wish to remind you of a fact that is, "A secret is only a secret until you tell the first carrier, then it is no longer a secret".

Whatever that is secretly being dumped into these environments will later influence you or your future ancestry, because there is a carrier who will take it to respectable communities.

When we look at the world and it being balanced out, poverty is of no disgrace and not everyone was meant to be rich or can even handle the pressure that comes with wealth. Personally, I often advised people that the environment that we labeled "The ghetto", communities of destruction, is also a street university and has been a road that helped lead many to success, depending on how you utilize the knowledge seen and given as you navigate those streets. Judge Greg Mathis is a prime example of that.

The negative responses we are seeing and getting from these welcoming facilities is highlighted as road blocks for those that dwell, and it will be if an individual allows it to be. Destruction and setback is in the mind of the person no matter what environment the live. But, if we document that negative energy into our minds, we can process it to be the motivational fuel that can drive us from homeless to Harvard and from ghetto high to the east side of town where we can get a piece of the pie.

We can be fully alerted and aware of what goes on in these neighborhoods without partaking in its negative enticements. But, if somehow we get caught up into these destructive lifestyles, whether it is because of hardship or disadvantage, don't get lost in its curriculum and rather design yourselves mentally with escape routs by keeping focused on a high school education, freedom from the clutches of the prison system, and allowing the activities around you to burn that fire beneath your dreams, talents and gifts; pray for strength to let go of those addictive curses and hold on to that ghetto diploma of street academics.

This strategy will alert the world that you have a story to share with another whom may have lost focus on life. With these escape plans you can beat the system, which was designed by man, whom categorized and placed humans into groups of "Good, better, best; to not so go, no body cares, and trailer trash".

The streets can and may take away our goals or it can propel the dreams of our children, depending on the seeds that were sown in the home and the magnitude of surface of which it falls on.

We must keep in mind that the "Streets we came out of withholds our secrets and the very same people we past by on our way up to success, will be persons we will once again, past on our way back down". We must not forget where we came from, because we are called to play major roles in the lives of misguided street teens and most of us, rich and poor, black and white, educated and dense came from these streets and know them best.

We can all be parents in the lives of teenagers whether they are our biological offspring or not. After all, true riches is not determined by the amount of financial wealth consumed by one, but by the amount of love we have and express for other human beings and how much we invest into their lives without expectations.

In the words of the Almighty God Himself (to each his own) who reminds us; "Our true treasures are stored in Heaven from the lives we invest our time, love and wealth in. Whatever we do for the sake of others, we do for Him". "We cannot say that we love God, whom we've never seen, but hate our neighbor, brother and enemy who you can see".

MY HOME!

Colors of laughter, a mixture of joy and pain,
Windows of sadness, tears like rain.
A touch of emotion, one can never pretend,
So deep are these thoughts, here in my heart therein.
Warmth and protection are pictures hung in every room,
These are the ties that bind, still as the man in the moon.
 I know I'm never alone,
As long as there's compassion and love in my home.

Laughter and pain,
Sunshine and rain.
Give or take,
Built ups or heartbreaks.
Sometimes together, other times alone,
These are the walls that make my house a home.

Never shall I comprehend,
I shall never pretend.
If I don't see, I won't try to imagine,
The secret thoughts these walls are keeping.
But in the midst of my profound thinking,
Are the thoughts so clear and thin.

Trouble comes and trouble goes,
If you don't speak, then how will I know.
I felt your pain, even if I didn't said so,
Because upward we stand, and together we'll grow.
No matter how I try, my house will never be a home,
Not unless Jesus' presence fills every room.

A HOUSE IS NOT A HOME!

What is a home?

Is it a beautiful decorated building with lots of luxurious designs, multi-million dollar paintings, stunning curb appeal and white picked fences; yet hosts day to day acts of abuse, battery, and molestation?

Maybe it is a place where kids have to parent themselves, because mom and dad are too busy working and doesn't have enough time to even share a smile with them in the mornings as they pick up a hot pocket before running out the door?

I guest it's a place where mom expresses most of her love to Marybeth, but neglect Johnny, making him to feel as though he has no value, stupid, worthless and useless to the body of humanity.

Maybe you called it a place where little boys and girls give up sleep each night to navigate the streets for purposes of prostitution; prostituting their frail bodies before returning home just before the sun is able to shadow the back of the ocean with a painful salary to help keep bills paid, a roof over their heads and food on their tables, while mom fastens herself in bed day after day to watch soap operas and dad is nick named The Story Teller as a result of frequent stories shared at nights around the table of barrooms after getting drunk.

Or; I believe it's that place where there's no form of civilization in the house; mother and daughter exchanges boyfriends and baby fathers, while father and son swaps technical knockouts, fighting like cats and dogs.

I believe some call it a place where secrecy is a member of the family and walls have taken oath of silence. They are restricted to share stories of little boys and girls are being used as sex toys for adults, encouraged by parents who are allowing the offense to maintain a blackmailed salary.

Whatever environment you construct your house, whatever concept you have in mind as it relates to the definition of a home, and whatever secrets you allow to be hidden in the cracks of the wall of your structure, I'll allow you to be the judge of what you make your home to be.

However you clarify or make meaning of that place, me being a victim of sexual, emotional, mental and physical abuse from houses governed by those who were suppose to protect, love and appreciate me, I can personally say that a home should be a dwelling place of love and togetherness; a safe keeping from the trouble and trials that grips the minds of innocence; the hurt and pain of day to day struggles, violence, kidnappers, sexual predators, and all the other battles that we experience in our lives, rather than places where we prefer to be any where else but a house that is not a home.

A child should never have to come to that point where they prefer to be dead; pushed to the limit where they locked themselves away in closets with knives and strings until their bodies are found without the gift of life's air, all because others felt that they were not qualified to be loved, respected and appreciated and as a result, victimized, bullied, teased and hammered them with slurs of derogatory nature, physically harm their bodies and manipulated their minds.

Death should not be the answer to putting a stop to gay and transgender bashings, derogatory slurs and teasing, long lasting abuse at school, neglect and sufferings at home, and being depicted as the class clown in rooms that should serve to expand one's intelligence.

Complaints filed against abusive attackers should encourage guidance to counsel perpetrators rather than victims. They are the ones with real problems. Inferior to others, they attack to become superior. They are those that are crying out for help, but their tears are not hands stretched out for assistance, it is through executing intolerant practices on those they consider to be weak and vulnerable.

Children should at no point be found buried in their bedrooms after passing out from prescription drug over dosages when had complained of repeated acts of rape and molestation that were conducted upon them by parents, friends and other family members, but having their voices go unheard, their tears unseen, and their signs neglected.

Our children should never be discovered hanging from beams of their school bathrooms by shoe laces, because they were laughed at in classrooms, pelt with food items in cafeterias and beaten in school halls and along walk ways by bullies, pushed aside and forgotten about by administration and teachers, all because they were afraid to address these troubling issues.

These are the places where children should be able to exhale, and if they aren't able to do it there, then someone please tell me where can they breathe after being boxed in by difficulties that life throws at them unexpected and daily?

Parents shouldn't be looked at by their children as the enemy rather than loving parents, unless it is for things that will protect them in their future. May Roper Coker said "Motherhood is the greatest privilege of life", and "A man who is ashamed of his family will have no luck", quoting the Yiddish Proverb.

This causes children to lose hope and give up on life; developing low self-esteem and forgetting their worth, eventually turning to drastic measures and abusing substances. When it get to that point, prepare yourselves for the worst, and I really do mean the worst, whether that worst is school shootings, domestic murders, an abundance of suicides, or them taking part in criminal senseless activities.

Experiencing domestic violence and sexual abuse by someone you love is some of the most painful and frightening conducts a victim could or should ever have to experience, and they should not have to suffer in such an abusive manner. No one have the right to sexually abuse anyone, even if it is done within marital vows, but more importantly; it should never be conducted and practice on children.

What has become even more disturbing, given its high frequency of occurrences, is the fact that many perpetrators of these violent acts are either family members or friends of these victims. This disturbing trend results in a loss of confidence and trust in loved ones, whom are closest to us. The people who share our homes, lives, and dinner tables with us daily are sometimes the most unpredictable, and persons who are "Mommy and daddy dearest".

The family is the basic unit and nucleus of any society; therefore violence, sexual and emotional abuse in the family undermines and rocks the security and fabric of any nation, and it's a known obstacle to social-economics its people.

Intolerant practices and violence is disturbing as it affects not only the abused victims, but also traumatizes the mindset of children in the home whom also experience physical, emotional and psychological scars from the exposure of domestic beatings and battering of a parents. Parents and family members suffer from the lost of fallen kids of murder/suicide. And the community that was forced a step back from being a better place as a result of a fallen nation builder and community activist.

Our innocent children are becoming more and more targeted and victimized, abused, beaten, assaulted and rape almost every second of every minute around the world by both male and female perpetrators alike, and are dying as a result of forbidden acts that are being practiced at school.

I must ask; how far we have to go before it's too much? How much do a child have take before they're able to defend themselves? And how many dreams of to be lost in order for us to wake up and take responsibility for our action?

We must examine ourselves and ask how far we are going to allow these kinds of violent attacks in our homes, whether they are parental attacks against our children, parents executing attacks on each other, or teenagers battering parents. How much lives have to be lost before schools would decide to fight for laws that will expel and forbid children that practice intolerance from ever entering another educational intuition as long as they breathe life's air in their bodies.

How many bodies do we have to find beaten lifeless hanging from fences and draped in closets before children learn to accept differences of color, race, religion, sexual gender and preferences? How many? How many? How many?

None of this is acceptable and it all have to cease immediately before we have a barbaric nation of children left without parents of domestic abuse or a society where the old grow and die without a generation to teach and reproduce.

What has become of our families, our homes, and our children? How did we become so careless, simply allowing the forces of evil to walk right in entrances of our dwelling places? How did we become so caught up with the glitters of this world, whereas anything becomes more important to us than the happiness and safe keeping of our children, our homes and families? Why are we allowing the media to home school our children with sexual perversion, violence and separation of brother and sisterly love, incest, drug usage and gang relations?

Whenever a child commits a violent act, take a look into their background and what you may discover may shock you. Wealthy parents deceive themselves into believing if they give their children whatever they ask or want, and the best of it all, they are being good parents. But, in reality, they are being some of the worst parents on the face of the earth. In fact, they are pointing their children into lifestyles that most likely will reap destruction in a sense, depending on how they allow those riches to manifold.

Don't misunderstand me; I'm not against children having things and there is nothing wrong with giving or wanting to give the best to our kids if that's what we desire to do. However, we must bless their lives in ways of which they can learn gratitude and appreciation for being able to have and enjoy the things we as fortunate parents are able to provide to them, and make them to understand and accept that advantage is never to trample on the weak or less fortunate, develop lazy habits or to abuse blessings, but to continue to push for independence and sow into others lives.

Children are being raised among families that live like wild animals where the strong survive and the weak get trample over. Yet, parents expect better when their children become adults, or are surprise to see their history in their children's eyes and display of behavior.

Parents cowardly isolate themselves from their parental responsibilities to raise their own children respectively, and rather use money, nannies, the media, the government and the streets not only as substitute parents, but as excuses for why they aren't able to carry out their duties.

These parental patterns pushes children away, isolates their minds from ambitious pursuits and spoil them into having their own way, which causes them to live according to the philosophy of their own minds. This mindset of unaccompanied thoughts, without adult supervision is a manuscript to kids becoming society rejects or potential convicts due to parental lazy and effortlessness to fulfill their purpose and responsibilities.

The face of crime and terror this day and time is not unknown to us, but comes almost as natural as the morning dawn. A knock on the front door can prevent dreams from coming to pass and unseen retirement plans. Toddlers in many of our cities and towns have heard so many gunshots and seen so many dead bodies that observing a blood covered fatal corpse laying along the street of their community is as common as the passing of vehicles.

Children are committing arm robberies at the age of ten; fifteen year olds are killing and being killed by adults and kids alike in cold blood; adult men and woman are graphically abusing toddlers sexually, even before their frail bodies develop; and parents are being battered by their infants in both upscale and rundown communities.

It is among and very familiar to us, so familiar that we tend to relax, allowing ourselves to be represented easy prey for those lurking to execute their wicked and heinous unspeakable acts of criminal violence upon us, which almost always begins in the home.

We have stopped depending on the protection of God and begun to lean on mercenaries; hired guns and weapons of mask destruction to fight our battles and solve our disputes. We refuse to parent our children from the manual God himself has given to us and allow the media to filter whatever they feel is necessary for teenagers to store into their brain files.

Our country's legislators have passed out laws to protect children from physical disciplinary action by their parents and school administrations, which left parents, teachers, administrations, and other children who want to learn open and vulnerable for violence, intolerant practices, teasing, slurs and battery to be executed on them.

There aren't many of our teens that have a genuine passion and concern about getting a good education in this twenty-first century. Sex, guns, and conflicts are the new thing for them. Little girls push to become early mothers with intent to burden the government with their responsibilities, while teenage boys with the absence of direction and ambition play the blocks, harassing and hurting others, before going home to a hot meal provided by the government.

I'm a product of poverty and came out of broken violent abusive tongue slashing homes and with the exception of infant minds; I can personally say that being a product of one doesn't have to dictate one's future. I held on to my dreams and refused to allow anyone to steal that from me. I wanted to live better and did all I can to become the successful gentlemen I am today.

Children and teenagers can and should fight that negative concept, because it is all in the mind and what they allow to digest into their system and channel into their heads will be what they will produce into society. Don't use the broken home/poor violent environment to be an excuse as to why you decided for yourself to be a convict or a product that communities of respectful people want to reject.

Parents should practice to uplift the spirits of their children by speaking positive uplifting words into their lives, without fail. They should consistently be reminded of who they are and what quality of life they possess. By remaining positive in their day to day life, in addition to consistently speaking positive words and keeping aware of the comments they make, it can build better parent/kids relationships, help communication skills, and encourages children to want to be better persons that their parents can be proud of.

Don't bash them with slurs of negative means or speak down to them, because the Bible warns that "The tongue is sharper than a two edged sword" and a parent words to a child can be just as lethal or worst. Whatever is said, can either make or break the future of child, all depending on the strength or weakness of whose brain processing the info.

Words are extremely powerful and essential to a child, depending on whose mouth it comes out of. Actress/comedian Mo'nique often reminds us of how as a child her father repeatedly told her she was beautiful. She held onto that and utilized that as a weapon to fight of the negatives that were thrown at her, because apart from her father's words, slurs and the way others viewed her did not mattered. She was a beautiful child then and she's a beautiful woman now, so the hell with the world and their opinions about her, and she will forever be a beautiful queen.

Writing from the lips of another one of our powerful black women in the world, Ms. Oprah Winfrey whom I not only love dearly, but one who has inspired me as a writer and motivator to misguided teens. She said as a child she was about to be placed into some form of reform school for girls, but when she was taken there, they didn't had an opening at the time. Because of that, she went to live with her father and by going to stay with him, it made all the difference in her life. Today, despite all that she has been through as it relates to her childhood, she walk with her head lifted high without any form of guilt or shame, and I along walk with her.

I love people in general, but children are especially precious to me. I love them with all of my heart and their lives are priceless, not only to me, but also to God who died for us all. We are the apple of His eyes, and as earthly parents we must make them to believe that they are worth living and even dying for. The perfect place to plant that seed is in your home, the foundation of the family; don't allow them or anyone else to destroy their will to live no matter who it may be.

The history of our country continues to be painted in bold majestic strokes upon a background of unsurpassed destruction. But, parents you are the artist and your home is your billboard; it is your obligation and you must demand and allow your brush to coat a different picture and broaden the base, upon which your children dwell.

Therefore; I have every confidence that although different affinities are in composition, the character of the people and the nature of their actions; the measure should be highlighted and addressed by our family's superiors and others in authority, along with members of the community, these troubling affects should and will be conceived, debated and resolved in its national interests.

I'M NO BODY'S CHILD!

As I was slowly passing by an orphan's home one day,
I stopped just for a moment to watch those children play.
A lonely boy was standing and I asked him why,
He then turned with eyes that could not see, and he began to cry.
I'm no body's child; I'm no body's child,
Just like a flower, I'm growing wild.
No mother's kisses and no father's smile,
Nobody loves me; I'm no body's child.

People come for children and take them for their own,
They all seem to pass me, Lord I'm left here on my own.
I know they'll like to take me, but when they see I'm blind,
They always take some other kid, and I'm left behind.

People see us children, and they think we're home,
They don't understand the pain, of being here all alone.
We know they're not our parents, and are only being kind,
But, Lord send me a family, one that I can call mine.

BE READY FOR THE FALL!

Love; a word that carries many meaning, such as the emotional passion, the physical intimacy and touch, acts of kindness, the desire for things and many more. However, the world's definition of love stands in stark contrast to God's take on the subject being our ultimate Father and a male figurative image. Young males especially have been bombarded with ridiculous notions of what love is really all about.

One writer said "Without parental guidance to form the walls of a straight and narrow path, children are destined for sudden destruction". As we can see, it is extremely hard to maintain the stability of the family and communities when fathers are disconnected from their families, leaving teenage boys to run the streets, while little girls dance in dolly houses with adult males.

Parents' visibility in their children's lives is most important between the ages of toddler to at least the age of twelve. At that age it is when they are becoming aware of whom they are, who their parents are, and their self worth, which will give parents the best opportunity to instill the qualities it would take for them to become respectable citizens of society.

Parents should not characterize love to their children only by going out and bringing in a paycheck or by giving them nice gifts, though these are okay. When an infant cries, the scent they should smell seconds later should be of that of their mother or a parent for that matter. They should be potty trained by the skill of their mother.

Parents should be visible in their lives to watch them take their first step, because it will be their introduction to society. When they look into the eyes of that stranger and make their first sound, it should be a cry for mama or dada, rather than for a nanny.

Children should learn their first letter of the ABC from their parents, because at that point they will be developing literature and the words their parents will say to them, will be of those they will take into the streets, school halls, and environment later on in their lives.

The first person that introduces a child to an educational institution and faculty should be that of a parent. And, the first set of teachers to introduce topics of sexual identity and sexuality, drugs, violence and morality, respect of elders and mannerism should be of that of their parents.

This doesn't just apply to those of the unknown, but also to persons of the rich and famous environments. I do understand the fact that at times parents have to be away from their children to keep a roof over their heads. Nonetheless, it shouldn't become the foundation of their family. Parents should never build their families on the pillows of finance, because if and when those pillows fail and those columns cave in, with it will fall the family.

Parents that are rich and famous, because of their financial status they are able to afford very good substitute parents, which are called "Nannies" to lend parental guidance to their kids or rather play that role of a visible parent in the lives they are being paid to babysit, and that's fine. However, we must remember those individuals, though maybe the most loving, sweet, compassionate group of persons on the face of the earth, they are being paid to conduct a service and your child/children is nothing more than a paycheck to them.

Even though a nanny may help them with their homework and see that they get hot meals throughout the day before being tucked into bed, there is nothing like that child's own parents putting their hearts into it; then it becomes an act of passion, love, and that sense of bonding between those parents and their child or children. After all, if money becomes the treasure of their parent's eyes and they continues to segregate themselves from their children and nannies display what parents should have expressed, compelling that bonding relationship to developed between them and those children, then they will become parents of your kids by love, time, and relationship; just without the bloodline to seal the deal. The actual parents will be considered only as those who planted eggs and gave birth.

I wish to warn and remind you parents that children have photographic memories along with mental recorders that snap and records whatever they vision and hear from behind the walls of their homes, which impacts their lives even into adulthood.

They live in a world far different from the one of which the older visionaries were raised in. Technology and knowledge is rapidly increasing as they swiftly mature physically, emotionally and mentally. Unfortunately, in these last days, the way they are being raised by the media, self-taught upbringings and kindergarten mind of intelligence, what they don't know can definitely and has often killed them.

It is statistically known that as children becomes of age, the influence of friends increases. This is why it is important that parents take full advantage of opportunities to instill as much qualities as possible into their lives while they are yet toddlers and at early stages of growth.

It is important for teens to chose their friends wisely and minimize the level of persons they group themselves with in order to avoid or decrease peer pressuring. However, it doesn't really matter how strong the influence is on a child; if their parents sow seeds on fertile soil, that tree of wisdom will definitely grow into their lives and will coach them into making good choices whenever they are challenged to demonstrate respectful decisions. This usually helps them to walk away if the pressure becomes unbearable.

Children must be able to feel safe under the wings of their parents and not in a war zone at home. They must not only feel comfortable with their parents, but also need to be comfortable with themselves. That sense of self trust should develop from within for them to be able to make good decisions sealed with respect and confidence between trusting adults and well instructed teens.

It is imperative for parents to instill that sense of value into their children, which will alert them of who they are, the quality of person they are and their self worth. Once that relationship has been established, parents wouldn't have to lose any sleep being concerned with their kids' decision making.

There is enough negative energy in the world within the destructive body of generational growth that our children don't need to experience these conflicting and incorrect information or display of action outside the home that the addition from parents is not needed.

Parents should serve as a safe haven of protection and backbone of support for their children to lead, guide and guard them from that lack of positive direction and guidance to such an alarming degree. They should know they are loved, cared for and appreciated in any or every circumstance by parents. They ought to discover their self worth at the earliest age possible. If a child begins to develop low self-esteem at an early stage of their lives, they will no doubt, take it into adulthood.

Our children's future is based upon whatever goes on inside the home. Their minds are photographers; whatever their eyes capture and is written on their mental files from behind the walls of their home and the display of action by parents; that mental influence will be taken into their adult life and possibly be past on to an unborn or infant generation, all because they lived their lives almost mirroring their parents.

Teen girls base their relationships with boys according to the way their fathers dealt with their mothers. Sadly, if they observe physical violence in their homes as children that were demonstrated on their mothers by their dads, they will end up dating men that will nine times out of ten, beat and abuse them.

They will develop that low self esteem deception and be deceived of the myth of violence executed on their mothers by their fathers expressed a form of love and affection in their personal way, especially if their mothers continued the relationship with their fathers. Therefore, they themselves, by being beaten, they are receiving that affection, and as a result, they become dependant on abuse to feel special and appreciated.

This was demonstrated in the case of singers Rihanna and Chris Brown a little while back. They were both megastars at the time of the confessed abuse, and many experts, friends, family members and supporters tried to coach her into getting out, because it is factually that if it happens once, it will predict the future. I agree with them, however, that is a lot easier said than done.

In normal cases, victims of low income would cling to the batterer as a result of disadvantage and dependencies. However, Rihanna is a young beautiful intelligent wealthy young unmarried lady without any kids who was not tied in any way to Chris Brown, so the question is, why did she struggled with going back and continuing the relationship with a man that seemed to want to kill her that night in the car; and thankfully she was in a public area at the time of the attack, because she might have been added to the list of fallen lovers.

Well the truth is, she didn't needed him for his pocket, because she is well able to support herself, she didn't needed him for the sake of any kids, because they had no kids, she didn't needed him for sex, because she could have gotten that from the best of the best out there, if I may say so myself. Rihanna didn't needed Chris Brown for anything else other than the little things that they had shared together when they first met and the emotional bond they had developed as it relates to their quality time shared.

She loved him and her heart was already caught up into the hurricane of affection with Chris Brown and that was what she wanted to return to. In a sense, what was shared between them during those special moments validated her passion, and I won't judge her for that, because she's a baby and still learning, and I've been in her exact shoes. It was extremely hard for her to leave him like I said, because she genuinely loved him. But, I'm glad she did, because I'm sure that night was not the first time he had hit her, and if she had stayed, he would have taken it to a level that would have dominated the last and killed her in an act of his uncontrolled rage.

As for Mr. Brown, I've lost the level of respect I had for him, because I feel as though he could have taken control of his anger and not allowing it to get to that extent for the sake of those who idolized him. But, I don't and won't judge him. Only he and Rihanna know what resulted his actions; therefore, I won't take sides. Nevertheless, I do hope that he would allow the experience of that night encourage him to get help fast, because he is racing down a path of sudden destruction.

Maybe the secrets that is hidden in Barbados in the closets of Rihanna's parents has contributed to her allowing herself to become a victim; I don't know, but this is what happens in homes where violence becomes a member of the family.

I know the role of a parent has become very challenging and critical, but children must be educated and informed of factual information. At no point they should be neglected, battered and or abused due to unskilled ignorant parents who don't understand how to coach, deal, communicate and properly prepare them for what they are expected to face in their future.

A dog knows love and if they can acknowledge love, how much more can a human being can acknowledge and appreciate. If we as parents continue to abuse, ridicule and drive our children away, while continuously expressing lack of affection and concern for them at every opportunity given, soon they will stray away to the blocks and run with anyone and everyone whose willing to accept, love, and appreciate them for who they are; and no doubt, they will be welcomed by those with manuals to street topics of drugs, crime, sex, prostitution, horrific violence, battery and even murder.

Once it gets to that point, it will almost be hopeless for that bond to be developed between them and their children. It would be as though they had given their children up to the streets and woman beaters, because they would lose all control of their family to professors of the streets who will parent them hard, and the child you once rejected, neglected and turned your backs on, you will regret in the future who they would become.

The street is a university that accepts all and rejects none, no matter the age. It is the only university that welcomes you without any credit, any grant and any tuition. It will treat you exactly the way you desire to be treated as long as you remain loyal and committed to it. You don't graduate from this university unless you are willing to sacrifice your life to pay the debt that you have accumulated for that acceptance and loyalty that was offered to you the day you enrolled. Although it is not impossible to get out, the debt that is owed is so hefty; banks refuse to give out loans to pay it.

This is when it will take the community to play essential roles to maintain, repair and assist into the reshaping and transformation of those teens; washing their minds and hearts from the filth and manipulations that would have been deposited into their lives, which can once again help them to accept themselves and enjoy the innocence of being teenagers and young adults that society can respect.

Parents should parent their children without compromise, but most important, lead by example. They must maintain that role of parenthood with a loving compassionate heart; but iron fist. They must be strong, bold, forceful and courageous; willing, ready and able to give their lives, if necessary for their children.

Without parental guidance to form the walls of a straight and narrow path, children will be lead to sudden destruction. However, this can only happen if parents neglect, batter, abuse and doesn't educate their children for what awaits their future. After all, "An ounce of prevention is worth far more than a pound of cure", and "The hand that rocks the cradle, rules the world".

If you rock that cradle the wrong way, our future generations will be nothing more than menaces of society. But, if it's rocked into paths of righteousness and with the principals of God, we will have Sirs and Madams of this world.

I know from the direction our country is headed, it may seem as if this modern generation is gone, but all is not yet gone, we can still renovate the minds of those who want to grow into respectful members of society. However, that results in us stepping up to the plate and investing ourselves into their lives with a no tolerance to fail attitude, which takes time to change the essence of a man, or in this case, a child.

FULL MOON!

You were my lady faithful and true,
Still I did you wrong, and now you're gone.
I'm sitting here hoping, that you would come back home.
While outside my window, there's a full moon.
If I can turn back the hands of time, you'll be rite here with me,
Making love in the moonlight, where we use to be.

There's a lot I can take, I'm a full grown man,
But, there's just one little thing, I can't stand.
I can't stand to see a full moon.
It brings bitter-sweet memories, now that you're gone.
I can't stand to see a full moon,
I'm so sorry baby, I've done you wrong.
There's a pain in my heart, now that you're gone,
Please forgive me, and come back home.

Since you've been gone, home is such a lonely place,
Yet all those sweet memories, I can't erase.
Girl I wish upon a star, and make my dreams come true,
And wherever you are, I hope you feel the same way too.

If I could turn back the hands of time, baby I would do you no wrong,
And you'll be rite in these loving arms, because that's where you belong.
I'm so sorry baby, I've done you wrong,
There's a pain in my heart, now that you're gone.
Please forgive me, and come back home.

DIVORCE

What is marriage, why do we get and should be married?

Marriage is a documented statement craftily designed by God, given to man as a guideline to not only maintain morality, but also self control, respect and honor in a relationship shared by two. It is a sacred vow that should be honored between once two individual uniting them as one; sealed with love, trust, commitment, blessings and faithfulness.

Marriage is something powerful and holy and when two stand with that agent of Christ, though they may have positioned themselves in the presence of a physical being, they really stood in the presence of God when they made that vow promising Him that they had desired to love honor and commit their bodies to the individual for the rest of their lives and is seeking His blessings to secure and protect the union.

However, if your intentions are cruel, don't get married, because God will not bless it for the fact that He is not in the business of throwing blessings away to swine when there are genuine people that can use and appreciate it. Therefore; we should not abuse the books sanctity by drunken ourselves with substances and uniting just because we can do it, for silly reasons and for lust or greed.

We shouldn't allow one night of laughter and erotic pleasure to bring home a lifetime of unhappiness, abuse, sufferings and demonic spirits, because that individual will forever be tied to your thoughts, your emotions, your character, and your will to build or be torn down.

In fairness to others, there are couples who get married as a result of partial love passion, and infatuation for there mates; however, this love seem to go no further than for better, but not for worst, because it appear as though the minute difficulty kicks in and the road get a bit rocky and hills challenges us to climb them, couples throw in the towel, forfeit the fight and bail on the marriage, not realizing the key and strength to any relationship is not really the good times, but the hard ones.

True love never lies and love tends to tests its authenticity. Genuine love is not the long hours on the phone whispering sweet nothings with butterflies tingling in each other's stomachs and the sharing of silent I love yous.

It is not the holding of hands in the shopping mall with the ten thousand dollar credit card limit and being able to afford items the eyes lusts after.

It is not about choosing between sittings at the dinner table deciding on whether to eat pan fried pork chops for a family dinner or if to go out to a five star restaurant and choosing the steak. Although it is good and beautiful that some couples can afford to do these things, that doesn't broadcast the strength of true love.

Authentic love is televised when the dairy of sweet nothings leaves the author with no more words to share and the butterflies are dead and gone from tingling stomachs; yet the fire of love keeps its glow in the relationship keeping that commitment committed.

It is when the few dollars is left home while husband and wife hold hands in the mall window shopping and wishing for days when they can bring it along with them to exchange it for gifts.

True love looks into the face of sickness and diversity and speaks to it, live or die; I'm here until then end. Finally, true love keeps that father providing for his family no matter what they are challenged with.

It is important to know whose hands we trust our relationship in when we decide to make that important marital step in our lives. We shouldn't allow any hired ceremonial conductor to speak into our lives their rehearsed speech and learnt words, because the blessings and words of God are essential for what awaits the future of the union.

The rate of divorce in our country has proven to us that after the drinking, the partying and dimming of lights, reality kicks in and the unknown identity of mates awakes from its sleep the dawn of a married day to captain our lives into the future, and sometimes they actually wears prada.

Another reason couples should not take their marital vows lightly is for the thought of their children's well being, if the marriage produces a family of kids or persons tends on adding to the union. As Judge Judy often say to her litigants; they picked who they decided to get with to have babies, but the children are those that are unfortunate, because they didn't chose their parents.

When unions are divided, children are the likely ones to get hurt the most and carry sometimes life long emotional scars as a result of bad decisions their parents made. Most don't consider kids feelings when they act the fool "Playing house" and who the real victims are.

Children aren't stupid, and depending on the magnitude of what takes place in the home, they know whether it would be necessary for their parents to separate/divorce or remain together to figure out their differences and work toward mending broken dreams and disrupted households.

Believe it or not, but children take their parents' marriage more serious than their parents do sometimes. Unlike them; they don't want to be without the presence of either party in their life. But, if they have to be torn away, allow it to be for reasons that are really unbearable, such as abusiveness, molestation or some form of drastic measure, because a child who is unable to bear the thought of a parent not being in their life sends them into a depressive state of mind, which influences substance abuse and encourages violence.

Teenagers should go through proper therapy to deal with the divorce of their parents, because all of that hurt, pain, anger and them being bombarded with confusing thoughts stored into their minds, with a fail attempt to get answers or the ability to reconcile their parents can be very devastating, and like a match that sit and wait to be scratch, so will be unprepared surprised youths of divorced parents.

The signs in most cases is often clear, but for puppy love, we often ignore them to remain in that passionate moment until it get to a point where our children have to be punished for our misjudgment and wrongful selection of character mates.

The key to it is to carefully monitor these signs at the earliest stage of the relationship so that it won't get too far ahead. But if, for some reason it does, privately pull them aside and talk it over, prepare them for the road ahead; at least by doing that they will be aware of it and can fix their minds to expect the unexpected.

I DON'T WANT TO HURT NO MORE

There are scars embedded on my heart,
Scars no one will ever see.
I have cried, oh a thousand times,
Since you've violated what was sacred to me.

Please show me how to ease the pain,
And how to make it go away.
Cause I'm hurting down here on the floor,
And I don't want to hurt no more.

I need a friend to hold me close,
And never, ever let me go.
To tell me everything will be alright,
Or tell me why mother had to go.

You said that love would come again,
You said that love's the only cure for the pain.
Yet, what was sacred, was taken from a child,
It's an everlasting pain, even if tomorrow brings you a smile.
I've felt pain many times, but not like this before,
And I don't want to hurt no more.

STRANGERS AMONG US

Everyone thought the gardener had done a wonderful job; the flowers were properly covered with matching colors that gave a magnificent expression of how the garden was beautifully done; but only time would tell its history.

Soon the cracks had managed to burst into a superficial covering. From thereon, in the beautiful splendor, it was all but gone. Everyone begin to notice the shatter in the petals of what they thought were an exceptionally well nursed garden. The fragile shell could no longer hold the growing rose; the silent cries of rape were no longer hushed. Over the years while no one listened and everyone seem to mind their own business, we soon realized that our enemy was not strangers at all, but those whom dwelled in our homes, slept beside us in our beds and ate at our dinner tables.

That once beautiful garden was violently disrupted when its roses could no longer contain the years of pain and frustration experienced in the home from day to day. The truth of the matter is, no one seems to have heard anything, and those who had heard, maintained their stillness; locking the secrets away.

We welcomed and accepted the abuse because we cage ourselves into a false world of "I can't allow people to know this is what had and is happening to me or my children", and by keeping silent, the internal truth of roses covered by the external beauty; we neglect the internal; despite it being in deep emotional pain.

The cycle of children being sexually abused and rape is almost becoming the norm among us. For every child molestation case we have heard about, there were ten that were swept under the mats by family, friends and others in society, including officers of the law and courts due to silence purchased by the almighty dollar.

This despicable behavior by perpetrators clearly expresses acts of cowardliness and disadvantage among those who lurk to trample on the weak and innocent; gaining their trust by capitalizing on their lack of convenience. Opportunity is at the forefront of their ulterior motives of sexual favor and practices.

It is extremely important for us to be aware of those patting us on our backs, eating at our dinner tables and sharing our homes, because many are not who they appear to be and are really not genuine friends and respected family members. Although we may know their names and they may look and act like us, behind shaded eyes they are those who awaits the opportunity to orchestrate heinous attacks and violations upon the innocence of our children.

I was a victim of molestation numerous times as a child after my mother separated from my father in 1982 and migrated to the city of Nassau, Bahamas after ten years of marriage at the tender age of three. This abuse continued on from three all the way to about fourteen by those of the known and unknown.

Nowadays; children are not being allowed to be children and are taking on roles of grown adults through sexual intercourse, pregnancy, prostitution, and parenthood. Their youth is also being ripped away from them through molestation done by sexual predators, which as a result, destroy parts of their emotions, their mentality and physical acceptance of who they are, and even with the best therapeutic interventions, they would never be the same.

There are approximately 45% of mothers who gave birth or became pregnant around the world while they were yet teens were raped, molested or bought by predators. 40% of our young men that are practicing homosexuals became confused of their sexuality after being molested the first time as little boys. This includes men and women, because please believe an adult female raping an infant boy can drive him to homosexuality.

These sexual curses are being placed upon them even by their own family members, friends of families and those holding public office; from churches to congress to classrooms, and many are aware of these sickening crimes, yet they sold their silence, not realizing the damages that is further being done.

The longer sexual abuse goes on, the more it robs the child of their will to love, their self esteem, their worth, their identity and their value; and if they know that their parents are aware, yet fail to intercede, they will lose all respect for them or whomever decided to have their silence bought.

The Bahamas; June 2009 at least twelve (12) junior high school students went into the summer break as pregnant teens between the age of twelve and fifteen. Although the Bahamas is dear to my heart and a beautiful place to dwell, it seem as though spread out among respected law abiding God reverenced citizens living on these great collection of rocks and keys there are thorns and thistles positioned that are blatantly abusing our nation's babies.

There are also those who cover it up whenever it tries to get into view of the public. They allow anything and everything to take place in this country, because its citizens are all friends from the politicians to the pulpits. As a result; as a born citizen of these seven hundred Bahamian islands and keys, I will personally say that Bahamians are partially responsible for a lot of their children's childhood and future being ripped away from them, not only by predators, but also by unfit uneducated slack mothers.

Deviance are preying down on their young sons and daughters, both willing and unwillingly, and some parents inside and outside of the Commonwealth of The Bahamas benefit just as much from predators as disadvantage children.

Many teenage mothers shred their young daughters' childhood by forcing them to take on motherly roles even before they are able to wash dishes. Because of this, it motivates them to carry themselves maturely the way adults do, eventually sexually experimenting until they are discovered pregnant by predators and dead beats, and the painful trend silently, yet blatantly continues.

A man whom I thought to be a respectable gentleman who I once rented from a few years ago in Nassau, Bahamas claimed that he had accepted Jesus Christ as his Lord and Savior, and by being one with more than most persons had, he started a little neighborhood ministry and food bank. He was a very nice person no doubt, and the tenants including myself couldn't ask for a better landlord to rent from.

As time went by, this particular gentleman rented a bedroom to a family that was struggling to make ends meet. I guest after later realizing that the father of five young children was a father struggling to make ends meet for his family, he allowed the mother who was uneducated and unemployed at the time to do odd jobs around the complex to cover their rent to release some of the burden that was on the family.

In addition to me, the parents of that family of five children, included a then eleven year old girl and his thirty-plus three hundred odd six-foot nephew who was a problematic unemployed repeated offender who was convicted of numerous crimes ranging from arm robberies to rapes and possibly murder, staying on that property living and breathing among us freely.

The nephew two years later raped that little thirteen year old girl. The mother of the child decided to prosecute the predator for attacking her daughter, but was soon faced with what should have been an easy decision to make. The landlord/uncle of the accused became aware of what his nephew had done and the charges that was about to be brought against him by the mother.

However, believe it or not, but that once highly respected gentlemen who had claimed to be a "Christian" that was ministering to many teenage boys in the neighborhood about God and violence turned to that disadvantaged mother and threatened if she did not drop those charges against his nephew she and her five children would have had to fine another place to live. Sadly, for the sake of convenience, that mother dropped those charges and allowed the creep to walk.

This story is really sad and unfortunately that little girl and others were forced experienced such a past as a result of disadvantage, but please believe that this type of behavior do not exist and condone only by those of the unknown poor inconvenient families, it is also demonstrated in a world of the known.

Persons such as Mary-Kay Letourneau and many others are being celebrated for acts that are considered criminal, which have influenced others to do it.

We have the opportunity to help the situation, but prefer to sit back, relax and continue to allow life to go on all because it is not taking place in our homes and to our families and children, or for the fact that we don't want to get our hands dirty.

But, if we are going to allow these high profile offenders to get away with heinous crimes, then we should apologize to every convict that is held captive behind the walls of the prison system; set them free and allow them to continue committing whatever offense they were convicted of.

If we're going to separate whose eligible or not to get away with crimes as a result of who they are or what their status is, then we should re-write the books of justice that would allow poor unknowns to die and famously wealthy others to continue living not being able to see their hands for the amount of sin that will be covering them.

It is a lot easier for girls to talk about being raped, molested or sexually violated than it is for boys to even think of such acts conducted upon them. And because of it, many predators go without prosecution and remain on the streets repeating pedophilic offenses.

After knowingly being violated the first time, teen boys immediately go into a state of depression and hence forth, live their lives in constant fair and denial, because even though it wasn't their fault that they were attacked and abused, the deceptive thought continuously play into their minds and confuses them into accepting the lie that they wanted, initiated and influenced the offense, or maybe there was something wrong with them which sent homosexual messages to their attacker.

I want you to picture a teenage boy locked inside a room with a sexual predator the way I was at fourteen years old, raping and molesting him constantly. With every chance he's given the opportunity to escape and alert someone of the attack, he doesn't as a result of guilt and shame. This sends an encouraging signal to his attacker who believes he's enjoying the acts and allows them to continue. But, he is not; he's simply afraid of what would happen to him and choices he would have to make as thoughts bombards his mind. So he keeps it in to protect his heart from further damages.

Although he may have protected himself from humiliation, harsh slurs, and teasing from friends and others in the community, he would be left vulnerable to his attacker and will remain in that compromising position with his abuser who most likely will be educating him of lies and deception that it is his fault and no one would believe it if anyone is alerted of the offense.

At fourteen I was placed into that situation. Most of my childhood I spent away from my biological parents and siblings, but at fourteen my biological father sent me to live with my mother in Nassau from one of the smaller islands of the Bahamas. Even then, I knew the nation's city was cruel, but my concept was based on violent crimes rather than sexual offenses.

When I got to Nassau and found that my mother by blood was living in a neighborhood where gunshots rang out at nights when birds was suppose to sing little children to sleep didn't surprised me, because based on intellect, she was unable to afford upscale safer environments so I fixed my mind to avoid altercations and interaction with persons that were influencing their captivity and freedom or death. However, what I wasn't prepared for and was not taught to protect myself from were sexual predators.

One morning a few months settling in, my mother got up and told me she was going five minutes down the road from where we lived to a short meeting and would return when it was over. I didn't think anything of it; I said ok and watched as she walked out of the door, closing the door behind her. I then jarred the door and settled onto the coach in the living room.

It wasn't more than ten minutes after my mother had left I heard a voice calling out from below the upstairs apartments. At first I didn't pay any attention to it, because people did that all the time. However, the voice was coming from below our front door with persistence, so I got up and walked over to see who was trying to communicate with us.

I stepped out onto the porch and saw what looked like a forty-plus two hundred odd pound man standing below our door looking straight into my eyes. The man asked in a pleasant, yet masculine voice if my mother was home, and I replied no. He said he needed to speak with her and asked where she went. I replied to a meeting and was expected to return shortly.

As I said before; I didn't know the stranger and had never seen him before for the fact that I was new to the neighborhood, island and surrounding environments, and he seemed to know my mother well the way he spoke, which was the reason for my extensive conversation with him. But, what should have raised red flags into my mind was when the foreigner asked if I was alone and insisted on coming upstairs and into the house to wait for her. However, it didn't; I guest because I expected better from him by the way he presented himself to me.

A thought did crossed my mind to not invite him upstairs being alone, but children of the Bahamas is taught to be respectful and courteous to adults, so hoping for the best, I invited him up and into my home. Although it happened more than sixteen years ago, I remember it as if it was yesterday, and will never forget the events of that day for as long as I'm alive.

I stood to the door to greet him and once he got there I turned my back to walk in front where I offered him a seat and something to drink. But however, to my surprise, the stranger wasn't behind; he walked into the house closed the door behind him and stood in front of it. At that point my heart started to beat and became overwhelmed with fear, though I didn't expressed it so that it wouldn't give him control over the atmosphere of fright.

I remained cool, calm and on my feet in the event I had to protect myself or scream out to neighboring persons. As the man stood to the door he begun asking questions, and the more questions he asked, the weirder it got. Finally he asked if I wanted a job for the summer break, and vulnerable to convenience, I told him yes.

The man then asked if I was strong, which seemed odd, but yet not strange, so I told him I was strong enough to do the work without even knowing what the work was. He smiled facetiously then shifted his eyes from my face to my penis area. He again asked how strong I was and if I was able to erect my organ to prove my strength and capability to him. At that point, my body begun to shake nervously as I said that I was unable to erect due to the tense situation at hand.

I guest at that point he saw fear in my eyes and decided to control the moment, because he kept smiling and insisting that I take it from my clothes and play with it until it erected. But, as frighten as I was, I told him I didn't wanted to expose myself to him.

The monster then walked from the door over to where I was standing and begun fondling me. After about three minutes of pleasure, he put his hand into his pocket, took out his wallet and gave six dollars to me as every hair on my head stood up with fear. Before he left, he told me that he was not a homosexual and that he was only checking me out for the job; but I knew better and I didn't argue, I just wanted him out of my house and away from me.

After the animal left the house and I was sure the doors were properly locked, I fell onto the sofa feeling dirty, ashamed; responsible for what had happened and deceived. Although I was molested many times before that, it was never by an adult male that seemed older than my father, whom I had trusted to not violate me the way he did. I wanted to cry, but couldn't find tears to shed. I wanted to fight, but felt I was responsible. I wanted to tell others what had happen, but couldn't find the courage and boldness to do so. I wanted to get up from the chair to scrub my body in a hot shower, but was too scorned to move. I simply sat there in complete silence for hours.

I felt so bad that I kept it all in and shared it for the first time at the age of twenty-five. This is only the third time ever since it happened that I'm telling it. That monster destroyed a part of me that morning. I lost trust in adults, and when I started dating, anytime an individual expressed their attraction for me to me that was older than I was, even as a young adult, it took me back to that moment; my body often shook and I got overwhelmed with fear.

I kept it from my family and the law, but protected and prevented myself from ever being caught in another compromising position ever again. I associated with adults, but always in plain view of others.

In this case, I didn't allow my attacker to repeat his offense on me; I'm sure he done it to others, but not on me. That was a very harsh fearful experience; it wasn't easy for me to share that and it is not easy for children to talk about molestation, especially little boys.

A child suffering at the hands of a predator and too frighten to alert others as a result of shame and embarrassment can and has often drove children to depression, suicide and even murder depending on repeat assaults, teasing, and shame.

It also causes them to feel very low of themselves, because I did. For others who tend to be weaker, they hold onto that guilt, even though it was not their fault. This drives them to engage in an abundance of sex with random partners, violent and criminal activities; wanting, needing, and desperately seeking love in all the wrong places. They also abuse substances such as drugs and alcohol to hide the truth of what had happen to them.

Death would eventually take its role, whether by self execution or abusing heavy substances, if one does not lend a shoulder to cry on, an ear to listen, a heart to express true love and compassion; lips to share words of encouragements to rebuild the walls of self-esteem that was destroyed as a result of abuse and sufferings; a voice to speak on their behalf, and a Bible to share the teachings of Jesus Christ.

The community must hold perpetrators responsible for their crimes, and should not protect them and their images, acquitting them by reasons of celebrity, marital vows or money, because at the end of the day, the real victims are those locking themselves away to commit suicides and taking our schools and household hostage to introduce death.

There are signs all around us and I want to say that we better start reading them, because if we don't, we won't be able to send our children to school or propel them out of our homes at all for the massive amount of sexual predators that will be preying and attacking them without any indication of fear or secrecy.

That creep boldly walked into my home with intent to molest me that morning, and it is that boldness that others have and will continue to attack other children. Therefore, it is imperative that the message is brought to the forefront of our society so that we can no longer close our eyes and continue to deny its existence.

I also wish to add that parents and the community should stop targeting and highlighting homosexuals as predators. They are not diseased animals and they are not monsters; before you attack your homosexual son or daughter, love them, because the lifestyle is the result of what may have transpired in their past that they didn't have courage to talk about.

A sexual predator or pedophile is not a homosexual or lesbian, though they may desire a specific sex. A homosexual is a man with emotional feelings of love for another male. The same is that of a lesbian. However, a predator is a predator, one who preys on children no matter the sex. They are individuals with desperate infatuated obsession of fantasies for children. So please, stop feeding the world with garbage.

Again; the signs are out there, the rocks are crying out and the portraits of blood painted pictures are hanging high on our walls of children that were murdered and had committed suicide as a result of secrets they took to the grave with them.

Dead bodies of our children are floating throughout campuses of our schools spelling the names of those failing to rest until justice revenge their deaths. It continues to send a clear message that lives are being lost and destroyed as a result of those who display themselves as lambs, but are really lions.

The jewel of our hearts should be found in our children; therefore we shouldn't allow anyone to violate them in any form or fashion no matter who they are or where they're from. Persons that rape, abuse and molest children, though we may know their names and watched them grow, we really don't know the identity of their intent, which makes them truly strangers among us.

ONLY ME!

If there is a beauty, you would ever wish to see,
The one standing in the mirror, is given the name me.
Tall, dark and handsome; son of a king,
For me and me alone, I'll do anything.
When friends and family are all hard to fine,
Deep within myself, I was the friend, God designed.
For you, my best, I'll try to do,
However; only to me, I can be forever true.

Hello; it is me, myself and I, three combine,
Me, myself and I; the one whom God designed.
Me, myself and I, is who I'll stay,
Twenty-four hours daily, seven days weekly, in every way.
Me, myself and I, I love me rich or poor,
This man standing in the mirror, I'm forever sure.

I am, who I am, it's all I can be,
Not him or her, just simply me.
For better or for worst, I can only live for me,
Whether I'm a doctor, lawyer, president, garbage collector or even thief.
When thunder erupts and raindrops fall,
It will have to be me, facing them all.

Take a look in the mirror; tell me who you see,
Is it them, or us? No, it's only me.
Like the air around us, as near as a heartbeat,
I must give thanks, because I was made complete.
I'll share my love with strangers and others,
But, I must accept me, myself and I, because we are brothers.

SELF WORTH

When God created the first man and placed him upon the earth, though he was the only human specie upon the land, he was positioned above all things, for the fact that he was made in the image of the Creator Himself and not called into existence like the animals, plants and other livestock were.

God later discovered His image lonely and in need of a mate that man could have identified with, shared similar characteristics and spoke the same language, so He took a part of His creation and made a woman. He ordered the female to submit under the authority of man, the first being, because she was made from a part of his body. However, she had her own identity and was uniquely created.

A few thousand years later, here we are a population of six and a quarter billion of us upon the earth. None of us are the same and no two persons are alike, even if they are identical twins. We all have different identities and were uniquely made, and for that reason alone, it make each and every one of us special and priceless beings. The value of our worth is far more than the purest undiscovered diamond hidden beneath the earth.

The brilliant minds of scientists and crafters can put a value on any and every man-made product created by humans, and even though physically they have categorized people and put them into groups of Good Better Best, separating them from Poor, Rejected and Trailer Trash; one can never truly put a factual value on a person's life.

We often see drug addicts, junkies and homeless folks begging and sleeping on our streets that we tend to write off as worthless, forgotten about and of no value. However, if we only had a single clue of how precious they are and how much God loves them, even to the point of giving His own life equally for them as He did for those holding the highest offices of our land, we will not treat them the way we do.

There are many people who we often pass on by and overlook because we don't see the potential in them. It is like Robert Downey's character in the "Soloist" that happened to stumbled on a violinist played by Mr. Jamie Foxx that had lost his way and helped him back to the man he was by expressing love, appreciation and friendship.

Love, acceptance and friendship re-lit the fire in that man's mind and encouraged him to bring his talent to the frontline where we can today celebrate his life.

That love, acceptance and appreciation Mrs. Gruell expressed to her class encouraged rejected neglected violent juniors to become Freedoms Writers. And love, appreciation, and acceptance kept a black man encouraged to continue the fight until he became victorious as the first black President of the United States of America.

Some of the greatest minds are held behind the prison walls; many are sleeping abandoned on the streets and have lost their way as a result of abusing substances. They have loosened grip on life, they have made mistakes, they made misjudgments, and they made poor decisions. Yet, they are alive and past mistakes don't invalidate potential. It doesn't destroy who they are inside and who they can still be.

Yes they have lost their way, but are sitting in front of statues playing two-stringed violins, sitting in classrooms with broken windows and torn books, and are fighting their brothers and sisters like dogs waiting on a Mr. Robert Downey Jr. and a Mrs. Gruel to extend their friendship, their love, their support and whisper to them with genuine belief that they are more than others value them to be and the world is patiently waiting to hear them play in the orchestra of new beginnings and read stories of unsurpassed truths.

Every man, woman, boy and girl were placed upon this earth with a capacity of intellectual abilities, crafts and skills, talents and dreams to help inhabit this earth in a way only we can individually. Though our Deoxyribonucleic acid (DNA) may not be the same, they are our brothers, sisters and children whom we should love, protect and encourage getting back onto the band wagon once they have fallen off.

Their weakness and mistake violates, prevents and robs the world and future generations of blessings, gifts, and nation builders. Don't criticize, trample down, and write them off. We need them and for the sake of an unborn or infant generation, we should lend ourselves to help build and rebuild them up so that the very purpose they were called to accomplish will be accomplished.

In the very words of Dr. Myles Munroe, the Bahamas' ambassador to the world who reminds us that, "The graveyard is wealthy with undiscovered talents, dreams, and goals that were never fulfilled. Many of whom were sent to help us with our goals". This is why it is our responsibility to fulfill our calling in helping to bring those dreams to light, and encourage others to identify their potential and purpose, because there are many who desperately depend upon us.

If you take a good look around your community, your society, your neighborhood and your country, you will find that it could have been in a much better state if only we had not robbed, discouraged, and allow the graveyard to steal our brothers and sisters that were still fighting and seeking ways to uncover their gifts and talents. This as a result, is affecting our lives, our communities, our society of people and our nation of children in many form and fashion.

Children all over the world are being murdered, committing suicides, prostituting themselves, strong out on drugs, and stricken with deadly deceases. They have lost their way, value and had forgotten or don't know what their potential is. They are responding to society the best way they know how to, which at times is violent and out of control. However, many of them don't know any other way and at times uses this behavioral pattern or strategy as a form of crying out to the community for help.

I'm curious to know who many of those teens that were shot down like dogs on our streets were suppose to be; what kind of potential they had, and what office they were suppose to hold. That we will never know, because to "Die with undiscovered potential and ability is irresponsible". In my opinion, it is the irresponsibility of parents and people society of to allow children to die with unused talents and gifts.

Everything in life was created with potential and possesses that possibility principle. Tragedy strike when a tree dies in a seed, an idea in a mind, a woman in a girl, and a man in a boy. For untold millions, visions dies unseen, plans dies unexecuted and future dies being buried into the past.

Solutions to problems of this world go unanswered, because potential remains buried. Some look, but others see, and what you may see, isn't all that there is. Potential is not what is, but what could be.

Children should understand that they are the creation of the Almighty God Himself. They are special and valuable and He loves them the way they are and there is nothing in this world they can possibly do to themselves that would entice God to love them any more than He already loves them right now the way they are. Parents should possess that same unconditional love for their children, because after all, they are earthly gods to their children.

They abuse their bodies by getting breast implants, facelifts, partaking in violent crimes and engaging in all sorts of sexual activities and tactics as a result of peer pressure. They live in a deceptive concept of the mind that the more they abuse and restructure their bodies, involve themselves in hazardous activities, and explore every avenue of sex, it would encourage insecure low self-esteem others to love, accept and appreciate them any more than they did before the sex, drugs, alcohol, implants, facelifts and violent acts.

Teenagers not realizing their value and worth suffer from very low self-esteem and they live their lives in a constant state of depression. They depend on the validation of others. If and when they don't feel validated, it develops hatred toward themselves, their bodies and others as a result of insecurity. They also often times lashes out in violence to express words they are unable to say.

Young girls usually engage in an abundance of sexual practices, while boys have a tendency to abuse and batter family members, substances such as drugs and alcohol, and play the blocks; all in attempt to find that love, wholeness, acceptance and validation; but in all the wrong places.

Unfortunately, adults whom are in position to help have a tendency to sit back and wait for hurting teens to cry us rivers of destruction before offering helping hands; then they point the finger of blame to isolate themselves from the problem of their own making.

But as for me; I don't have time to listen to rehearsed sympathetic speeches when schools are being held hostage, actors are being shot dead in their vehicles, fashion designers are being fatally shot as they exercise, and athletes are being killed at gas stations and in their homes. There are hundreds if not thousands of signs that point in the direction of hurting persons and 99.9% of the time someone is aware of what's going on, but as always, ignore them until we have to wash their blood of the street.

If we would only stop for a moment, look around and listen to the voices in the air that tries to warn us of what lies ahead, we will no doubt, see that there are many hurting teenagers and people out there who are suffering and desperately crying out for our help in many different areas.

Apart from the normal day to day struggles of starvation and homelessness, many are suffering from a lack of love, covering, protection, physical, mental and sexual abuses, emptiness, insecurity, and lack of support.

Many are voluntarily offering themselves to engage in sexual activities with men, woman and boys, not because they are in love with these individuals in most cases, but as a result of them feeling as though they may never find love again if they don't advertise and market their bodies to those expressing interest that has proven to be brief and bitter-sweet. They parade themselves for attention, not realizing they are doing more harm to themselves by giving up their bodies than good.

This behavior results in females experiencing a magnitude of abuse in relationships, many of them are not strangers to most of us. By them not getting that love or knowing what true love is, abuse seem normal and beatings translates as an expression of appreciation.

Teenage males react in a form of rebellious and immoral behavior, partaking in sexual practices with young girls and boys voluntarily and involuntarily, which results in them being dead beat dads of children spread out between many mothers or suffering from diseases they contracted as a result of their homosexual promiscuous lifestyle.

The rape and molestation of our children's hearts, character and innocence has become normal to those adjusting themselves to these heinous acts and deviant practices.   Predators are filtering themselves into our schools, church halls and scout organizations; all for the purpose of preying on vulnerable children. As a result of neglect and abandonment, they turn to violence and other sources of death.

This concludes my point; teenagers experiencing such past don't feel good about themselves and hold strongly to thoughts of worthlessness. Therefore, they feel they have no value and have nothing to really live for or seek after. This mindset, in addition to many other levels of abuse and conflicting information can and has often translate into murder/suicide or both when pressure fills the pipe, resulting in an explosion.

YOUNG LIVES!

Children are my friends,
They love me and I love them.
Some mornings down at the seaside,
We sing songs, as they pass by.
Gentle are their smiles,
Laughing together; what innocence in a little child.
Love them, and then stay for awhile,
Great is God's faithfulness, in the eyes of a child.

Sing children sing,
There's no need to worry or to fear a thing.
Life with its cross and crowns,
Can sometimes build up or break you down.
Fly children fly,
Life is beautiful, just look into their eyes.
Sing for me, sweet melodies,
Be free to love, laugh and dream.

Heartache and pain; push them aside,
Please know life is like the ocean's tide.
Sometimes low, other times high,
However it flows, go for the ride.
Black, white, rich or poor, it don't make a difference,
God loves you and treasures your innocence.

FORCES FROM WITHIN

Loneliness is not as easy to bear as it may seem; everyone wants to know and feel that they are loved and appreciated. When that affection is neglected or lack, it robs happiness, laughter and even tend to destroy self-esteem, and as a result, pushes the individual to seek love, want and acceptance in all the wrong places. First come, first served; whether it is homo or heterosexuality, it won't matter, just as long as they are being loved.

It is extremely hard for most, but meanly children to go through life not experiencing or even being able to express love, and being treated as an outcast further sinks them into depression as it relates to unwantedness, rejection and loneliness.

I'm familiar to this, because I personally experienced it. For that reason, I highly respect teenagers who were bullied at school and in their environment, yet graduated with good grades and moved on with their lives to become respectable productive members of society, instead of turning to drastic measures of retaliation or revenge throwing it all away as intended by perpetrators.

It should not surprise parents that most victims of intolerance prefer to privately deal with their problems rather than bringing them and others into the matter for as long as they are able to endure the abuse and sufferings, which they feel might increase once administrative action is taken.

Though this is an easier solution and may prevent a wave of panic among parental bodies, by them withholding information of their abuse from parents and at times school administration, it manipulates them into believing that all is going well with them at school, which in many cases have turned out to be the complete opposite after they are discovered dead by means of suicide or they take a school hostage and commit murder.

The surprise discovery or act of death in the past have left many parents speechless and with a number of unanswered questions as it relates to the cause of triggering of violence. However, parents maintain that deception as a result of not investing sufficient time into their children's daily lives to distinguish whether they are hurting or not, and I guest that is why children withhold things from them.

Although it is true that children are not sent to school to be accepted and love, but to rather learn; a loving and accepting environment helps children learn better if they know they are appreciated, because it is humanly impossible for one to spend five to ten years in an educational environment and come out successfully not being loved and fairly treated or having to defend themselves of repeated intolerant attacks.

Apart from intolerant practices, today we live in an age where children are coming out of school and entering this global economical market hosted by technology unskilled and unqualified. Many of them are still reading at kindergarten levels, speaking in a language the market rejects, and not mentally prepared to be dedicated to employment that cannot make them instant millionaires.

This Twenty-First Century is an age where manhood is important and as a result, due to insecurity, teenagers react first and think later. They are not going through proper channels of their lives from the cradle to the classrooms, and with an angry world with a thirst for blood; uneducated, unskilled, insecure teens left unsupervised by neglected parents is vulnerable to its hand's reach.

They are killing out each other; are we noticing that? Prisons are being built and gutted to hold our babies; graveyards are running out of spaces, and grandmothers are sleeping with guns under their pillows in fear of a generation that threatens them from living out their lives and retirement plans.

Parents should not expect success from their children if they are not willing to spend an hour in the evenings to help their kids to become better readers. Mothers should not expect for their daughters to love and appreciate their bodies and prevent men and boys from abusing it if they don't give a moment of their time to remind them of their worth and sacred virtue.

Fathers should not expect to see their sons become gentlemen, bread providers and nation builders if they continue to separate themselves from their families; leaving them to roam the streets at night. They should hang their heads in shame when the courts sentence their sons to prison, because it is as a result of their invisibility that most teenage boys go astray.

Teens being taught of their self worth from loving homes understand who they are from within, and that helps them to look at life differently. If this modern generation of mothers would only adapt the attitude of yesterday's generation where parents picked up at nights where teachers left off during the day and repeat the cycle, this world can and will be a better place to be and grandfathers could go back to sitting on their porch to enjoy the sunlight and the cool of the blowing breeze as they read the news paper.

A child at home may be the apple of their parents' eyes, but at school and on the streets where no one know or even care to know who they are, love or compel to love, appreciate and accept them, it is a different ballgame played and the very place they were sent for a valuable purpose or the environment of which they live can be a safe haven or a war zone, depending on how the crowd welcomes them and the skill of problem solving they transport into society.

In a world of their peers, no one really cares who they are or where they came from, and sure don't care whether they live or die. Therefore, it is an absolute urgency that parents evaluate themselves and pencil a none negotiable time into their schedule to taking their children back from the grips of the streets, the strong hold of the prison system, drugs and alcohol, violence and demonic forces.

There are a lot of teenagers in this world who do not have an opinion of their own, transport very low self-esteem qualities and depend on others validating them. They live their lives depending on our every word others say to them due to the way they feel about themselves. The same way we can uplift their thoughts and enhance their spirits, encouraging them to love their bodies and work hard toward success, we can break their strength, cause them to lose hope and give up on life.

Homosexual and lesbian teens not being able to express themselves or live comfortable lifestyles among their peers also have a tendency to commit suicide. Although it is not known for homosexual teens to commit murder; they soon will if they are constantly beaten, victimized and have their advantage taken. They will commit murder only for the purpose of revenge, but will turn to suicide to escape the emotional stress and painful abuse of bashing and hateful slurs.

On April 20th 1999 the two young men of Columbine High and many others that had committed murder/suicide were not targeting specific victims, although they might have shot and killed a few they may have known and observed as the enemy.

There were no special selection of victims on that day, the victims were whoever was present and post a threat of getting into their way of accomplishing their goal of making a statement to the world.

This kind of violence is called "Illness-Base Violence" where once again there is no special selection of victims; the victims are those present during their reaction of anger and rage. Their angry mentality influences them to dominate by all means necessary, to always remain in control after being neglected, rejected and most likely abused in order for them to have a voice.

A gun in the hands of a marine symbolizes protection and a defensive sign to external threats. But, a gun in the hands of a teen symbolizes power, control and revenge. A wave of violence is sweeping nations across the world's blood paved surface. Guns are dominating our streets, and it takes nothing for a brother to take the life of another from a different mother.

Children cry out for help in the voice they know, which is known, but unspecified to ordinary minds, whatever it may be. However, despite its tinted picture, the message is clearly painted. Therefore, if we wish to stop or turn the tap of this gushing faucet of bloodshed to a dripping valve, we have to collectively work in a systematical order and do what we can as one people with one goal and defeat strong holds of intolerance, hate and bigotry.

Again, it's important for parents to dedicate their time and energy into knowing where their kids are at night. Legislators have to develop a no tolerant attitude and put forth laws that will make examples of those that attack others with hateful words and slurs, violence and threats against race, preference and gender. It is also important for teachers to be in a safe secure environment so that they can teach our nation's youth adopting the attitude of Mrs. Eron Gruel.

The difference between a standup youth and one with no direction is the environment. Children understands even at their earliest stages of growth that having a gun in their hands flips the script of power and control on those they fear; that is the reason why many want it and most are in possession of one.

A children as young as four, with a gun in their hand controls the power of life and death, and when they are in that position, the thrill of controlling the atmosphere of fear elevates them another level of high.

Power turns a coward into a man and a lamb into a lion. It turns a kitten into a tiger, a student with a history of straight A's into a serial killer, a caring friend into a coldhearted monster and a selfish mayor into one that abuses the people of their community, which they truly enjoys for as long as it lasts.

There are signs and billboards throughout the world warning people, but especially teens of the results drinking and driving causes, because alcohol and vehicles is like the countries of Iraq and Iran; one day they are together and other times America has to referee one from slaughtering the other nation of people.

However, it is the same way with unmonitored teens without parents and problem solving communication skills. It is the responsibility of a parent/guardian to know the whereabouts of their children as long they are dead and in the hands of the law. If a parent cannot give an account for a child and their action, that parent should be equally prosecuted if neglect or abandonment is proven.

Teens are fighting the greatest fight in the history of the existence of this world. Those who choose not to fight are trying to escape by abusing substances of drugs and alcohol. They are searching high and low for that distant love of lost and missing mothers and fathers, and believed that the abundance of sex will bring closure to that empty hole in their hearts. But, as a result, they are further destroying their priceless quality, their worth, their value, and are rapidly being wiped out by deadly diseases.

The battle against stress and depression compels children to war against themselves, their parents, and respectable members of society for the fact that they don't want to face troubling issues and don't know how to handle painful thoughts. This causes them to abuse drugs and alcohol which serves as substitute parents that takes it all in and make them feel good until they deflate from that invincible high.

They live in a age filled with media-based fallacies, and if the message isn't clear enough, Ill be one of the many to tell them a public secret that depression, stress, and loneliness hate substances like drugs and alcohol with a passion, and statistics have testified that when they are forced to greet, they usually destroy those that brought them together, whether it is by persons committing acts of violence, hurting themselves or having violence committed on them; either way, someone is going to be punish as a result of them not having control of their minds.

Our children are uniting these individual products to its complete dosage for the mere reason of escaping from a familiar world of violence and abuse of various kinds. Poverty and hardship is also a depressing factor that is no doubt causing them to commit violent crimes against themselves and a nation that should be preparing an infant generation of what sleeps their future. If we continue to neglect our responsibilities given to us by God who asks us to show them a better way; then we should have no tongue to criticize them, because we would have defeated our purposes.

We can all make a difference in their lives one at a time, but only if we try. We shouldn't be quick to judge and condemn them or others even when they commit these magnitude of violent crimes and senseless acts, because in the very words of my mentor Miss. Oprah Winfrey who said "I realized all pain is the same, all heartache is the same and all anger is the same; this was what they (whomever) chose to do with theirs, so I wont judge them".

This point brings me to the conclusion; teenagers experiencing a history of unimagined unthinkable abuse, abandonment, attacks and violations don't feel good about their lives and hold strongly to thoughts of worthlessness. They usually feel unvalued, unwanted and unappreciated. At that point, dreams are given up, songs go unwritten and unsung, medications go undiscovered, and graveyards expand its walls to receive lifeless talents.

I've personally walked through this valley and gave all I could have in attempt to rebuild the structure of character, self-esteem and self-worth that was lost or violated by others whom had snatched the innocence of their youth. I continue to fight for innocence and I pray that by my words of encouragement, we would stop for a moment to collect our thoughts and question whether we really want to continue living in a world of neglected broken out of control barbaric generations and generations to come. If that answer is no, then invest an hour of undivided time into a child, a neighborhood of broken people, and a community that seem to be abandoned and forgotten about by the government and other sources of opportunity.

Help transform and rebuild their mentally broken structure. Though this may take a very long time, the goal can and will be accomplished. It is our individual responsibility to be our brother's keeper to help one another realize and appreciate the value God has placed on us all that is simply priceless.

Again quoting from the lips of a mentor, Miss. Oprah Winfrey who shared after returning from a trip to Africa, "The people of this world don't have the slightest idea where this world is headed and what will be its outcome. If we don't help these hurting children now, then we'll all suffer the consequences later. Because, it's not just these people and their problems; it is people who live in the same world as us and their problems, and we must help them".

Our very future is inherited by a generation of youthful minds and characters, we as older visionaries were called to guide and direct them into paths of righteousness. We must fulfill that calling rather than expanding the problem by raping and abusing their intellect.

THE EGO OF THE DAMN!

Thus proceeds the earthly men of ego,
The so called statesman, churchman and holy being of self.
Regaled in illusion, they embrace the conclusion, "Me, myself and I, see us grow.
Violence prevails, but for them, they say all is fine with wealth.
However, that claim is decline,
A simple case of the blind painting negative signs.

They have site, but no vision to the powers that be,
Though they have eyes, they yet refuse to see.
Blinded by their arrogance, they say I'm god; I'll lead this race,
But at this moment; their heart beat, next breath and another day, only by God's grace.
Jokes people, know that God is not to be mocked you fools,
Arrogant holders of deception, embracing illusion and looking cool.

The realm of His spirit, is your true home; God loves you,
Give love to all, justice to all, and then to thyself, and please be true.
For this is God's world joker, not ours,
He created us His children, my selfishly ignorant brothers.
Remember, He hath scattered the proud for the conceit in their hearts,
He hath put down the mighty from their seats, to repent or to depart.

BULLETS & THE BIBLE!

This smile broadcast on my face is a beautified deceptive expression of all the things that I try to hide. I hid the time I was seven when my dad threw my mom to the floor and beat her like a stray animal caught into the pen of chickens raised by southern farmers.

I hid when I lost my innocence early to an adult I did not love or offered myself to. I hid the pain I felt when it happened. I hid the regrets of trusting those I thought would protect me. I wish that I would die.

I held these painful thoughts inside masked beneath my perfect smile. I hid my true feelings toward what people had said about me behind my back, determined not to let them see me fall apart.

I hid the fact that my life isn't as beautiful as people think it is when I'm in the spotlight. I also hide loneliness and emptiness that constantly battles with the joy I truly wish to feel inside. I'm fighting to not breakdown and cry; I've heard so many lies and gotten so many empty promises.

I smile to hide the disappointment that I feel from constantly being let down, victimized and taken advantage of. Everyday of my life I wish that I can walk away from these memories that I have; it's so much pain, so much regret and so much hurt, the only thing that I can do is hide them beneath a smile that is built on a weak foundation.

Hypocrisy has made a name in the churches and is painting signs, wonders and mistrust to youths and lost souls; pushing them further and further into the grips of Hell, rather than directing them into paths of righteousness.

Religious leaders are more concerned of their large member body, having their faces painted across television screens for the purpose of raping Christ Jesus' body of its virtue; all to sign autographs, transport themselves in the best vanity is offering, and to eat at tables of canal beings of earthly value, instead of going out into the highways and byways to seek the lost, the hurting and the dying without notice.

Men are going home from night clubs and barrooms at night to beat and abuse their wives, rape their children and shy from the wealth of fatherhood in exchange for adultery, homosexual practices and substance abuse.

Young woman and girls are prostituting themselves, neglecting their children and succumbing to dangerous drugs, while men and boys are committing violent crimes, dropping out of schools by the minute, and committing suicides as so called "Ministers of the gospel" are busy on golf courses.

They are more worried about their crafty egoistical message being presented in a fashionable manner, than keeping themselves humble and clarify the word of God whereas a child that is alone tucked away in a closet somewhere listening to his television set could understand the truth of Jesus and reconsider putting that noose around their neck and saving their lives. Yet, they wonder why our youths are missing from the church family.

Religious leaders delivers messages from pulpits a number of times a week highlighting sins of others; yet at night they creep around their wives, partake in sexual and homosexual practices with young boys and girls, batter their spouses and are abusing substances worst than admitted alcoholics.

They dress themselves in the best designer suit and ties, jewelry that gives competition to the sun, and speak quoting the best scriptures ever written in the Bible; though their hearts are hallow and filled with lies.

Eternal life that Jesus Himself has given to us freely is being sold to the highest bidder, all because those whom had trained their minds and spirits to the teaching of truth are filled with desperate yearnings for the wealth of this world. They quench their faith and weakened their strength to heal and cast out demonic forces such as racism and homosexuality. As a result of their inability to properly perform acts of the Holy Spirit, they sit back and condemn sinners for the honest way they live their lives true to who they are.

Religious leaders are so caught up trying to please themselves that they forget to notice the fact that our young men prefer to run to the streets where they use guns, knives, and other weapons as tools to problem solving, while females are prostituting their bodies to feed their babies instead of seeking the assistance of the church, because those whose tears don't go unseen and ignored, others have to exchange sexual favors with pastors or have doors slammed in their faces.

Night after night children go from bad homes to bad streets to bad schools, all in bad environments and back again as a result of abandonment and neglect. Those who are able or in position to help prefer to lock themselves away at nights, leaving them to die on blood washed streets.

Most of our youths who inhabits run down neighborhoods are often denied opportunities as a result of where they are and how little they have, which gives them not much of a choice but to run the streets at night, steal due to starvation or for survival, and rob innocent others of their honest earnings, while churches spend hundreds of thousands of dollars on stained glass windows and luxury vacations in stead of investing it where it is really needed.

Homosexual practices, sexual engagements, dangerous drug usage and other monstrous habits is acceptable to engaged in behind the walls of our schools, while others go on suspensions, even being expelled for thirty second to one minute prayers of thanks said to God for another day of life and over their meals in cafeterias and classrooms.

Hate and bigotry against sexual preferences and race is practiced religiously in our communities, schools and among families, and persons are constantly beaten, violated and have their right to live peaceful acceptable lifestyles in a country that claims to be free taken away, while students expressing their love and relationship with Jesus Christ is threatened to cease or face expulsion.

One of the founding fathers of America left a blueprint of future warnings, saying "It is impossible to govern the United States of America without the principals of the Bible". Yet, there are teachers, administrators and politicians observing and referring to the Bible and its teachings as a book of witchcraft and hate speeches.

Rappers and rock-n-role artists are teaching children how to commit murder or to rather use violence as solutions to conflicts, engage in sexual practices, and abuse dangerous drugs and are getting through to them, while others are fighting school boards to be allowed to pray in school.

There are teachers, school bus drivers and other faculty members that observes little boys and girls engage in oral sex on buses and in classrooms, even partaking themselves, while the law of the land is busy pulling the name of God out of prayer to please students that seem to practice black magic and none religious groups.

Self proclaimed Anti-Christ representative, rocker Marilyn Mason walked on stage at an award show and in the presences of millions, if not billions of teenagers worldwide, destroyed a Bible and cursed the name of the Almighty God. That was considered fun and entertaining to on lookers as they clapped and cheered. However, the world was ready to condemn Ms. Janet Jackson to Hell for exposing a little breast for a performance gone bad, which wasn't even her fault.

Rock stars and even educators are educating youths on how to commit suicide professionally and they deceive them of a dangerous myth that it is okay to sell their souls to Satan for a life of fame, fortune, sexual perversions, unlimited drug usage and none stop parties. Yet, the churches are cowardly sitting on their mouths and allowing our teenagers to walk through valleys of shadows of death without a friend to guide, protect and pull them out from the clutches of these demonic deceptive strong holds and agents of evil.

Religious leaders of other faiths are teaching their members to distant themselves from the teachings of Jehovah's Witnesses; however, they don't have the slightest drop of courage to go into areas where families sleep on their floors, young mothers creep to stovetops to prepare meals for their children in fear of getting hit by stray bullets that frequently travels throughout the neighborhood and buildings that are designed by the skill of riddled bullets.

These are places Jehovah's Witnesses discover themselves day in and day out, I guest holding on to that confidence that their leader, whoever it may be, will protect them from all harm, while other faiths remain under their umbrella of protection in million-dollar structure continuing to minister to seat warmers.

It seems as though the script has been flipped, and those with the greatest authority one can ever posses are allowing evil to dominate us quite and blatantly. However, as the question is often asked; "If God is all powerful and all loving, then why would he allow children to go without food, teens to kill and destroy communities of people, and hurricanes to destroy lives?

On the 20th April, 1999 two young men walked into their school and shorten the lives of twelve students and a teacher before turning the gun on themselves, destroying lives across an open scale.

The question is; where was God when the victims of Columbine High School needed Him?

On September 11th, 2001 the world mourned as a nineteen men team of hijackers made history when they confiscated four major airliners and used them as deadly weapons; crashing two into the twin towers, one into the Pentagon and another into an open field; thank God for the brave men on the final flight who was courageous enough to give their lives to save many at its intended target.

When it was all said and done on that horrific day of bloodshed, a little less than three thousand lives were lost, many innocent children are today without parents, and millions of hearts were left forever scared.

The question is; where was God on September 11th, 2001 when the victims of the twin towers and all that was trapped into the belly of those planes needed Him?

On the 28th December, 2004 a Tsunami struck the Indonesian district, washing over three hundred and fifty thousand lives into the valley of dry bones, while leaving millions of children and families around the world scared and asking questions.

Again; my question to you is; where was God when the earth shifted sending thirty foot waves crashing into small towns and villages that had inhabited millions of people?

On Monday April 16th, 2007 a young man walked into Virginia Technical College with intent to kill as many as possible and a mindset to be carried back out in a body bag by strangers. When his mission was accomplished, thirty-two young lives lay dead.

I ask yet once more, where was God when teachers and students were overwhelmed with fear barricaded by trapped doors and sealed windows needed Him?

The answer to all of those questions is; He was rite where He has been ever since the beginning of creation. He remains with those who are for Him and against those who are against Him.

God is a god of mercy, love and of compassion; there isn't anything in or out of this world that is too good for Him to bless us with, neither is there any evil He wish to have harm us. This was proven to us when He turned His head on His own son over two thousand years ago, allowing Him to suffer and die for sins He did not commit, when man should have died.

Yet the question remains; where was this all powerful, all loving God and why is He allowing young brothers to be shot down in the streets at night like dogs; sisters and mothers to be raped, victimized and murdered in their homes and on the streets in attempt to make a dollar to feed their families and children dying by the thousand as a result of poverty and heartbreaking diseases?

Well, from the very lips of Mr. Pat Bone himself, God speaks:

"Who; the God we doesn't want in our classrooms? The God we don't want our children to pray to? The God we are taking out of our homes, schools and law books? Is that the same God we're asking to protect us from harm?"

Billy Graham's daughter added to that when she was interviewed on the

Early Show and Jane Clayson asked "How God could let something like this happen?", shortly after the September 11th attacks.

Anne Graham-Lots thought for a moment and then gave an extremely profound and insightful response. She said "I believe God is deeply saddened by this, just as we are. But, for years we've been telling God to get out of our schools, to get out of our government and to get out of our lives, and being the gentleman that He is, I believe He has calmly backed out.

How can we expect God to give us His blessing and His protection if we demand that He leave us alone?" Mrs. Anne Graham-Lots couldn't have given a better response.

In light of recent events, terrorist attacks, school shootings and others that had and continues to plague our lives, I think it started when Madeleine Murray O'Hare (she was murdered, her body found recently) complained she didn't wanted prayer in our schools, and we said Ok.

Then someone said you better not read the Bible in schools, the Bible says "Thou shall not kill, thou shall not steal, and love your neighbor as yourself", and we said Ok.

Then Dr. Benjamin Spock said we shouldn't spank our children when they misbehave, because their little personalities would be warped and we might damage their self-esteem (Dr. Spock's son committed suicide). We said an expert should know what he's talking about, and we said Ok. Now here we are today, after submitting to the opinion of man rather than the warnings of God, troubled by the consequences of our actions.

This resulted into a reversed prayer written by an unidentified little Ohio boy who prays; since the Pledge of Allegiance and the Lord's Prayer is not allowed into American schools anymore, because the word 'God' is mentioned:

"Now I sit me down in school,
Where praying is against the rule.
For this great nation under God,
Finds mention of Him very odd.
If scriptures now the class recites,
It violates the Bill of Rights.
And anytime my head I bow,
Becomes a Federal matter now.
Our hair can be purple, orange or green,
That's no offense; it's a freedom scene.
The law is specific, the law is precise,

And prayers spoken aloud are a serious vice.
For praying in a public hall,
Might offend someone with no faith at all.
In silence alone we must meditate,
God's name is prohibited by the state.
We are allowed to curse and dress like freaks;
Pierce our noses, tongues and cheeks.
They have outlawed guns, but first, the Bible,
To quote the Good Book makes me liable.

We can elect a pregnant senior queen,
And the unwed daddy; our senior king.
It is inappropriate to teach right from wrong;
We're taught that such judgments do not belong.
We can get our condoms and birth controls,
Study witchcraft, vampires and totem poles.
But, the Ten Commandments are not allowed,
No word of God must reach this crowd.
It is scary here I must confess,
When chaos reigns, the school's a mess.
So, Lord this silent plea I make,
Should I be shot; my soul, please take. Amen

Today we're asking ourselves why our children have no conscience, why they don't know right from wrong, and why it doesn't bother them to kill strangers, their parents, classmates and themselves; probably if we had thought about it long and hard enough, we can figure it out. I think it has a great deal to do with us reaping what we had sowed.

It is funny how simple it is for people to trash God and then wonder why the world's going to Hell. It is disturbing how we believe what newspapers and media reporting says, but question what is written into the Bible.

It is also mind boggling that people send jokes and other gossips through emails and they spread like wildfire, but when messages regarding the Lord are sent, people think twice before sharing them.

It is frightening how lewd and lascivious, crude, vulgar and obscene articles pass freely through cyberspaces without question, but public discussions of God is suppressed in the schools, workplaces and ends up into junk mail.

I guest some may say slavery isn't as bad as driving a major aircraft into mega structures to destroy lives, but just a few short years ago blacks and Hispanics were beaten, raped, spat on, degraded, disrespected and killed; all for simply being of another color and race. They hadn't done anything wrong and were not as fortunate to request differences in skin color from God before being birth into this world. They were given those skin colors and birth into those races as a result of God wanting them to be that way. Yet, their lives were ripped away from them in graphically heinous methods.

My question to you is; was that in the will of God who made those people to have their innocent lives ripped away like that, when he specifically told us not to commit murder?

No, it was not, but people did it anyway and felt that it was right and fair to do, both then and now, even with laws that are in place to prevent these types of behavior.

People had no mercy as they tied up innocent men, woman and children to lamp pools burning them alive in the streets as crowds of families of the same race cheered and danced the night away.

Ku Klux Klan members enjoyed the thrill of torching thousands of families out of their homes, vehicles and businesses; forcing them to go elsewhere. God and the church was their only refuge as they walked through valleys of shadows of death. Yet, it is that same God who was neglected, rejected, forgotten about and asked out of our lives, our schools, prayer and families, while others who worshipped Him were pulled out of sanctuaries by hate groups and beaten.

Boys and girls were raped, beaten and killed by other races. However, God was watching and he convinced Dr. Martin Luther King, Jr. and others that though revenge was not theirs to take, their deaths would not be in vain, their cries would not go unheard and their sufferings would not go unpaid for. Today I'm sorry to have to say, but I think He's repaying those whom violated His anointed ones right about now.

I must say that the magnitude of attacks on others by hate groups has been tuned down. Nonetheless, it still exists. Racism and bigotry still lives and breathes among families across the earth's surface by pass generations whom still believes the color of one's skin should determine their measure, and again; it's filtering back into the lives of teenagers from behind the walls of their homes, such as the radically self-proclaimed Pastor Phelps and his family, straining into our schools, streets and work places.

Violence is at its peek in our country; almost daily our teenagers are using knives, guns and other destructive weapons to use on other students, family members and strangers alike without hesitation of ending their lives.

The question today is; where are the churches when we need them?

Teenagers are feeling so low about themselves that they are turning to suicide, prostitution and dangerous drugs more often than before. They are being neglected by their families and are afraid of being kidnapped and sexually assaulted by those presenting themselves as angels of light.

The answer is the church is in hiding and is looking out for self pleasuring, while those such as pimps, drug lords and leaders of gangs are lending their shoulders and arms of protection to our children, until they are no longer of use to themselves or death becomes them.

Those who are called by God to direct His people are afraid to get their hands dirty standing up to the giants of this world. I must warn those whom are using the teachings of God for self gratifications that there are many hurting people out there in this world who depends on every word from that very Bible; if we are going to minister to them from that book, do it with sincerity and in honesty, because if we deceive them, their blood will stain our hands forever and we will no doubt, answer to God for leading them astray.

Children are looking for someone to look up to, something to run to, and a faith to believe in; they are being welcomed and accepted by all, except by those who claimed to be called by God for that purpose. However, if we, the church body who seem to be convinced that Jesus Christ is the one and only don't allow our lights to brightly shine into the pitch of darkness, then our Lord Jesus' death was in vain, our practices of faith and belief is only a mockery to His resurrection, and we are blaspheming against Him by exalting ourselves.

We cannot pimp God, we cannot neglect and throw Him away when things are going well with us, but expect Him to help and protect us against the evil we open our very doors to and when the weight of the world falls on our shoulders.

We cannot make ourselves gods of wealth and riches, yet expect the Almighty to cover us from sudden destructions when He clearly asked us not to make unto ourselves graven images.

We cannot expect to insult our Lord Jesus in plays painting our Savior as a practicing homosexual engaging in sexual perversions with His twelve disciples and expect Him to cover us with His mercy and grace.

We must understand that God has made us in His image and likeness; therefore, as humans grieve and hurt over painful words and gossip said about them, God have feelings too and He also hurt and understand the same way we do and we should not expect to be bless and protected if we are going to treat Him and His feelings any way we wish.

Yes; He loves us with a love that is never ending, a passion that one cannot put into words, and covers us with grace that continues to bring us through day after day. But, He will not stand and be insulted, rejected and disrespected, because He don't deserves it, and this is why He allows things to take place at times to prove to us that He will not allow us to use His love as a sign of weakness and give a green light to take advantage of Him.

What transpired in the history of our experiences was allowed for us to learn, and we should sooner or later learn that God is merciful and of great love and compassion, yes; but He is also a fair and just God, whatever we ask for we will receive, whatever we do to others, will be returned to us triple fold. Therefore, if we wish to erase Him out of our lives to live by the sword, opening our hearts to evil forces, then those very fruit will be returned to us, and like Mrs. Anne Graham-Lots said to Ms. Jane Clayson, "God; being the gentlemen that He is, He will no doubt, calmly back out of our lives and leave as defenseless as we desire to be.

It is imperative that prayer and other Godly principals be put back into our lives, our schools, in our functions, and in our law books. Prayer changes things and I beckon to President Obama who openly professes his faith and following of Christianity to please put God and prayer back into the schools, remove the law that restricts parents from disciplining their children and pass laws that favors people more than profits, and watch the turn around of your nation's youth and people.

Satan is walking upon this land with one goal in mind, and that goal is to "Kill, steal and destroy", whatever was implemented by God to prevent His reign and the abolishing of evil is in his favor. However, he is defeated, but until the end of the earth, it is his will to do whatever he can to prevent his sufferings and it don't matter how young or old, he is corrupting the minds of the young to destroy the fundamentals of the adults, and the mature to destroy the adolescent.

God was put into our constitution, into our courtrooms and into our schools so that we can be govern by justifiable godly principles. It is therefore, important that we go back to that old fashion way of putting God first or else we shouldn't have anything to say and allow ourselves to drown in the blood of innocent others.

This is harsh to say, but it is the truth and if we don't do something now, these will be our words of regret in the very near future:

"I sit here writing my thoughts on your mirror; I sit here crying what is left of my life away. If I had only give a little of my time and told you how much I had cared, you might still be here today.

Although you didn't go by my hands, I took your life away. I thought I knew what you needed, by giving what I believed you wanted. But, for things, you didn't give a damn.

I'm in a constant state of depression, beating on my chest to see if I still can feel, and through it all, I see reflections of you lying on the floor of your classroom dead, where they left you, after it was over.

I'm crying away my fears, and I'll regret my neglect until my dying day. I'm sorry I took your life away, I don't know why I was too busy for you my child, I guest I wanted you to have the finer things that I didn't had when I was your age; scared of poverty. Don't haunt me please, because I can't reply. All of this regret is already killing me inside.

I'm broken inside; my heart has turned into glass. I was fragile until you took your own life; I'm broken inside like a dropped crystal vase. I'm tattered, my wings won't let me fly; I lay here every anniversary of your death and cry, because I know I might be the reason you died".

Jesus said, "If you are ashamed of me, I will be ashamed of you before my Father that is in Heaven".

PERSEVERE

When I was yet a young boy, mother use to say,
Learn all you can child, prepare for a rainy day.
Please stay in school boy, listen to what the teacher say,
This point from the royal leader will help you on your way.
To drive a nail right son, hit it on the head,
Strike with all your might child, while the eye is red.
When you get work to do boy, you must do it with a will,
Those who reached the top child, had to first climb the hill.

Standing at the foot son, gazing at the sky,
How will you get up boy, if you never try?
Though you may stumble off child, don't feed of cast,
Try and try again boy, you'll succeed at last.
Don't be a rude boy; it won't help in any way,
Study real hard son, someday it's going to pay.
Don't you ever stop boy, remember what mama say,
Cause you'll fine a mean world, waiting to play.

Even goals may same hard boy, but don't give up the fight,
Keep hammering away son, you'll sure to get it rite.
Resist peer pressure child, you don't have to be like the boys,
Explore your own arising, it's bound to bring you joy.

Reach in your soul,
Set a positive goal.
Then follow through,
In whatever you do.
Son aim real high,
There's no limit to the sky.
Don't waste your mind,
Cause it's only little time

SOCIETY OF HOPE

Violence as we all are aware may occur in any home, school or organization; sometimes smoldering, other times blazing catastrophically; but it always destroys various aspects of our lives and community.

The direct effect of this flaming fire of violence is usually experienced by survivors, such as teenagers of murdered parents, parents of falling children, and families of suicide victims; many of whom, in most cases, did not kindled the flame, but all that were burnt by the fire.

Individuals not being held accountable or responsible for their violent behavior, intolerant practices of slurs, teasing, and bullying, in addition to those with out of control explosive tempers increases the level of attacks and lost of lives.

Persons or perpetrators with these personalities tattooed to their character are desperate victims with desperate means or need to control, those that are lacking and seeking attention, love and affection, and persons with hidden secrets that interfere with their happiness. As a result of their personal internal battle, they rage war against others in attempt to find peace, comfort and joy.

Perpetrators responsible for stealing others' joy are victims themselves despite the fact that they might be to blame for raping persons of their happiness and even lives. They are victims because if not for what may have happened in their childhood, issues with low-self esteem, loneliness or depression as a result of unknown affection and appreciation, they most likely would not treat persons that are not at fault for their inner problem the way they do.

Perpetrators or responsible victims as I would call them, until they get over or resolve that personal matter hidden in their life's history that consistently tend to rage war with their happiness, or issues they may be forced to face at home in their day to day lives, they will forever discover fault in others for the fact that they live they lives transporting yesterday's baggage.

The baggage that responsible victims allow to shadow them highlight fault in all except them. They tend to hold everyone accountable for their hidden secrets and mental war. They bash homosexuals with words and physical attacks because their lifestyle, in someway mirrors what may have transpired in their past or continues to plague their future.

They beat on their partners, wives, siblings and mothers because they may wish not to be controlled or might hold them responsible for not protecting them the way they felt was good enough. They fight against authorities and programs that are in place to help rid their future of history's baggage, because it is a lot easier to hide and carry them around than it is to face it. And, when no one is around for them to explode on or bash with cruel words, they abuse substances.

As you can see folks, it is nothing personal between responsible victims and those that are innocent; it's the internal battle that they are running from, which propels them to paint you as an individual of issues. They are crying out for help in the tongue they know. But, for those who wish to continue to hold on to their problem, drugs and alcohol is for the purpose of excusing their bad behavior and to continue their violent reckless activities. Once this is discovered, it becomes the responsibility of the law to through the book of justice at them without compromise.

We live in an age of darkness; a world that is filled with fear, hate and intolerance, and our children are falling victim to these crude acts. Many of whom are being robbed of their youthful innocence to enjoy who they are, while others lives are being shorten by violence, sicknesses as a result of drugs, prostitution and promiscuously sexual behavior.

A number of them are rapidly turning to the streets for support they seek from homes and schools. Schools that suppose to serve as learning facilities and safe havens have become war zones as it relates to violence that is being executed behind beautifully painted walls and million-dollar structures.

They worry themselves more about getting back and forth from home to the battlefield safely rather than concerning themselves as they should on academics.

We often complain about school violence, but don't bother to discover root causes of escalating aggression, at least not until it is too late and many lives are affected and possibly lost.

The cause of escalating violence in our schools and on our streets is primarily the result of intolerance of anyone who is different in anyway from what society depicts is normal among our youths, people, especially neglected teens rejected and abandoned by parents and the community and from a lack of opportunity.

Intolerance has to cease wherever it is practice throughout the world. Bullying, hazing, teasing and the vicious attacks on homosexuals is some of what attributes to violence and should not for any reason be tolerated period.

The way children interact with each other and the way they treat others should be addressed first and foremost. The attitude of everyone involved, such as the law, teachers, principals, and administrators must change. It is also imperative that the mindset and lack of concern by parents change and they must pay more attention to signs that highlights pain and suffering in their kids' eyes.

Children should be taught while they are yet young how to respect, speak, treat and be considerate of others and their feelings when they interact with those in their age bracket and older. They should not practice humiliating, harassing, physically and emotionally abusing others while they are kindergartens, because those habits will graduate with them and enroll into higher learning facilities, which certainly will be executed on those they interact with on a day to day base.

The media is manipulating our children and treating them like puppet on strings. They are brainwashed into believing that their lives and self worth is of no value unless they engage in the abundance of sex, abuse substances and bully others that seem to be weak. Because of this, they are living reckless lives to be a part of that something; whatever it may be.

People, especially children in our communities are really hurting, but are very talented. Yet they are lacking opportunities. Hurricane Katrina was sent to the Golf Coast, not necessary to kill, steal or destroy, but rather to unveil painful secrets of those living in poverty; communities that were rejected, abandon and struggling families in neighborhoods that were badly hurting, but kept from the viewing public, which gave reasons to contributing violence and the many lost of lives in those low-line areas.

I know for a fact that people only pretend to care until they are put to the test, because this has been proven throughout the ages. The Government and most of the organization that claim to be associations for helping people, manipulate the people year after year, term after term, day after day with bullshit promises that has to be fulfilled.

I was an out of controlled teen a few years back as a result of what had transpired in my life's history. I wasn't gang banging or engaging in any hardcore criminal activities, but I was one that needed a guiding light, and later got that in the body of my friend, father-figure and mentor; a wonderful human being that is known to the world as Dr. Davidson L. Hepburn. One of my nation builder, he caught me before my getting caught up with the wrong crowd.

Before meeting Dr. Hepburn and displaying qualities of rejection, throughout the years I observed my mother threw her complete support and fight hard knocking on doors, shouting, screaming and going many nights without sleep to elect time after time The Progressive Liberal Party (PLP) to office. However, once they took office, they neglected her and brushed her off as if she was lint on an expensive suit.

Many boasted of her dedication to the party and representative, yet she and her children, which included me went days without eating, wore a lot of hand down clothing, and migrated throughout the community as a result of inability to afford decent housing; and those we did found and were able to afford were many with outdoor toilet and sanitary facilities. Thank God for His grace that brought us through those difficult times of our lives.

Those experiences drove me to dream of being many things as a teen growing up in disadvantaged communities that had lost many of its youths to violent acts. But, when I finalized my future and chose a career, I settled on one that would be of help to humanity, after identifying gifts of speaking and creative writing that God had given to me.

I penned this book, disturbed by what was going on in the lives of the generation I'm a part of and those that were behind. I understood the generation that was before me, though might have loosened its grip of strictness throughout the ages leading to my birth, they had still deposited enough quality to me and others to be handed down to one that was unborn or in infancy as they journeyed out their lives and retired to their place of rest.

Therefore, I knew if me and others like myself didn't got a grip on those that have not yet gone astray and teach them what we were taught; sad will be the cry of a people that will shadow the growth of my generation.

As a result of an unknown identity in the literary industry, I independently published this book, which resulted in a lot of out of pocket expenses. At the time, I was employed by the Government of the Commonwealth of the Bahamas as a General Service Worker making less than twelve thousand dollars a year.

In attempt to live a reasonable honest lifestyle with the salary I was obtaining and to cover out of pocket expenses, I took out loans at a local Bahamian bank to finance all cost of the manuscript to the actual book form and proofing status.

I got to the point of where it was being processed for release, but had ran out of funds to further cover technical costs and moneys for promotion before the time I was pushing for its launch. I was in a jam and needed additional moneys, but my bank was refusing to extend the loan and others had tightened up on giving out and consolidating loans due to the economic decline as it related to the global recession, which was understandable.

I became frustrated and frantic; I needed that money and desperately wanted my book to release. As a result, kicking or screaming, I had to come up with the funds to meet deadlines to compensate the then summer of two thousand nine launch date. But, as it neared, I became more and more frustrated and worried about the money and tried many ways of getting it, but to no avail. Every avenue I went to became dead ends.

Another local bank decided to consolidate it, but as quickly as I had gotten my hopes up; it fell to the ground as it related to getting the funds, because I didn't have assets that were valuable enough for them to hold as collateral.

I applied for grants that was intended to "Help" ambitious youths to jumpstart goals and entrepreneurial ideas, but was turned down due to claims of insufficient allocated government funds.

I applied to the country's development bank, which was again put in place to supposedly develop and give back to the people of the Bahamas; but was turned down as a result of not having valuable items of collateral. At that point, disappointment begun to creep in and I started feeling more and more let down. Yet, I continued knocking on doors and pushing further to get assistance.

I then, giving the fact that I was an employee of the government, wrote, met and spoke with seven (7) government ministers (Members of Parliament), including the Member with responsibility for Education, the Minister responsible for Youth, Sports and Culture, the Member responsible for National Security and the Prime and Deputy Prime Ministers of the Commonwealth of the Bahamas.

I displayed the physical proof copy of the book and told each of them what my goal and intent was as a young Bahamian. I said to them that as we look at what is happening in our country and around the world today as it related to violent crimes and teens committing tem, it was my intent to go and fight for youths all around the world, but as a native of the Bahamas, I wanted to use my life as a positive template for others to emulate, and hopefully by accomplishing my goals as a Bahamian internationally known author in my youth, it would encourage and inspire other Bahamian teens to follow their dreams rather than chasing after the negatives of the streets.

I told them if we wanted to take guns and knives out from children's hands and prevent them from using it on each other and other members of society, we must first be prepared to exchange weapons with opportunities, because we cannot expect to take what they know without giving them something better.

It is unfair to ask them to stop protecting and handling issues they are facing, the way they know how, yet neglect and abandon them, leaving them idol and vulnerable to violence and struggles without knowing any other respectful way of dealing with it. That is like taking bleach from the reach of a baby, preventing them from being hurt for that moment, but without being removed from the area and exchanging the bleach to a toy or a bottle of juice, leaving them in the environment of gasoline where it is accessible for them to play with or drink; they will go after it and destruction/death will follow.

I didn't ask for gifts or handouts, but a loan with intent to repay within a matter of months following my book's release in addition to giving my time freely to speak, which I'll still do to my nation's youths and assist in the rebuilding of the country.

I sat with the Minister with responsibility for the Nation's National security, and given the position our country is presently in as it relates to crimes and idol teens committing them, I figured he would have been supportive to me as an ambitious youths. But unfortunately, as expected, he said he was unable to assist me.

The Minister of Education, though there were countless murders, sexual abuse cases and stabbings done to and by students on his watch and even on school premises, you would have thought he would have considered helping; but he didn't answered my letter and refused to spear me a moment of his precious time, despite the fact that he and I worked in the same building and only a wall away from each other.

The Minister with responsibility for Youth, Sport and Culture, though the book is with intent to help encourage youths to put down the guns and knives; mature from boys to respectable men, and repositioned themselves back into their place of fatherhood to single parent sons, he gave the same response to my letter as others did of his inability to help.

The Prime Minister didn't replied at all, despite two letters sent to his office and one placed directly into his wife's hand who currently serves as a senior high school principal. However, the Deputy Prime Minister responded through the voice of his secretary who told me on behalf of the honorable minister, there was nothing that he was able to do.

I wish to remind you that I didn't ask for gifts, but a loan from seven very wealthy powerful men whom were in position to turned stones into bread, but refused despite that my cause was good and my intent was to credit the Bahamas; my country, their country, the country whose people, including youths had supported them to offices they will hold until the first quarter of two thousand and twelve.

I was humbly at their mercy and begging for a crutch as a wounded soldier until I was able to stand on my fight in a territory that seemed to be taken over by domestic thugs and barbarians.

I was begging for an opportunity to help my country when monsters were breaking into little old ladies houses robbing, beating, and murdering them. I knocked on their doors and asked for an opportunity to help the citizens of the Bahamas who was in fear to sleep at nights when sixteen, fourteen and twelve year olds were being murdered every other day in schools, on basketball parks and on the sidewalk as they sit to chat with friends at nights.

I was begging for an opportunity to make the Bahamas a better, more financially secured place so that seventy-nines and eighty-five year olds could have enjoyed their innocence and retire to the beach or prayer meetings rather exhausting away at vending boots and petty shops where they are vulnerable to being attacked and beating for a few dollars.

I was fighting the Government of the Bahamas for an opportunity when thugs were kicking down doors at nights and murdering innocent others in their bedrooms as they slept. I also was begging their financial compassion when school boys were falling to their knees in tears as they shared painful stories of teachers who were drugging and raping them in classrooms, impregnating little girls before they get to know themselves and children whose innocence were being bought and stolen by teachers that were abusing them.

Finally; I was begging for an opportunity to help encourage fellow Bahamians to put down the guns and knives so that law abiding respectful youths like myself and others would not have to walk the road with eyes pinned in front and back in fear of being attack, or sleep with weapons at our bedside in the event our doors are kicked in and thugs attempted to harm us. Yet, all seven semi and filthy rich of them slammed shut their doors to me and the people of the Bahamas.

The hurtful thing about it is, the bank of which I was in debt to as a result of previous loans previously owed is owned by the Deputy Prime Minister of the Bahamas, who is also a multi-millionaire. Nonetheless, it was too much for him to authorize an extension to a loan I was already paying on to help a good cause.

The way I look at it, even if they couldn't help, which they could have, but had each pushed their hands into their pockets and had given me a dollar a piece; they would have donated to my cause, contributed to the youths of the Bahamas, and expressed encouragement and appreciation for my positive attempts. But clearly they don't care.

I unfortunately did not make my summer release and was forced to postpone to the Thanksgiving season as a result of the setback, but this experience had given me a reason to give sympathy to those that had committed themselves to the streets and practicing habits of crimes.

Teens aren't stupid, just misguided. They know politicians, most of them, are bullshitters. They can see night and day between genuine concerns and brush-offs. They know, despite what is fed to the viewing public that the government looks out for their own and has abandoned others to the streets where they kill out each other fighting like cats and dogs; this is why they have developed that "Don't care" attitude and hatred for the world and display their wrath on whomever crosses their path, which as a result, keeps positive brothers like me in fear for my life and restricted from befriending certain environments.

I was very hurt of the way I was treated when I meant well and was trying hard to help the people of a country that is very dear to my heart. However, I shouldn't have been surprise, because from generation to generation, the behavior of Bahamian politicians has remained the same. They knock down doors for their family members and themselves to give help and donations to many who don't need it; neglect those who are really in need and hurting; but use these same people to get back in office time and time again. This is why for the thirty years that I have been on the earth and in native of the Commonwealth of The Bahamas, I have never voted for either party, but hoping for the day I am voted to the office of the Prime Minister to change this deceptive manipulative trend.

It is factual that most of us don't pay attention to anything unless it directly affects our lives, which is sad and depressing. But, I want you to understand, especially politicians that no matter where we go or who we security ourselves from, violence knows no race, no color, it is not afraid of power and it doesn't care for riches. It reaches to the very distance no matter how open or secluded of an environment.

If we really want to protect ourselves from this wave of angry violence that is sweeping across our nation, especially in the world of this nation's youths, we must first put a stop to intolerance, hate and bigotry and live our lives as vehicles of love to others; bless their lives with opportunities and stop putting them into character boxes of separation. Be a society that cares about people rather than money and things and go back to the days where five loaves of bread and two fishes were offered to feed a "Ghetto" of hungry families.

DIFFERENCES OF WHO WE ARE

"No two persons are alike", this remains the same throughout the ages of time. However, I'm a uniquely created educated human being; yet I'm disrespected and disenfranchised for a color I did not choose for myself. This too will continuously migrate itself into the age of our future, carried by persons set in their ways and refusing to change their habit of thinking, their practice of hate and their pattern of separation and divide.

But, I refuse to change, despite people's thoughts of me; my complexion doesn't define the character of my being, and I'll say it and I'll say it loud; I'm Black, Hispanic, Caucasian, Asian and I'm proud.

Look at me, today I stand before your presence and serve you with dignity and grace. I nourish your soul with words from a spring of living water of life and inspiration, uplifting you emotional and mentally to a pedestal that is served by those of great distinction.

I am one to be respected, presumably for what you can see in the light that displays my character, which backsplashes the rear of the sun. However, in a rey of that same light, when the moon cools the evening and fear is dominated by bravery; here I lay married to a pavement whose foundation stabilizes the structure of a bar, drunk to disgrace out of a conscious mind like a sailboat tossing and turning violently as it defends itself from a raging storm.

In the midst of the battle, when my thoughts regrets giving way to my flesh's selfish greed and continuous thirst for more alcohol, with that nasty feeling, but a sober mind, I pray for the hangover to quickly past me by and promised never again, that it would be the last. Nonetheless, the moment I'm released from the incarceration of drunkenness, I find myself back in the moment, and the saga continues.

Look at him, Mr. Ralph Lauren, a fashion mogul, a gentleman with a humble spirit; one who is deserving of respect. He dresses nice; he certainly is attractive, smart and successful. I like him. However, I too am a fashion explorer; I'm a designer of my own style and taste, and though some may picture me as ugly, that's a matter of their opinion that they deserve to have; I too deserve respect and appreciation for being me.

The considerable "Weird and freakish" are persons that are different from what society depicts as "Normal". The way I shave my head, the black clothes that I wear, and the way I choose to live my life is my chosen style of beauty, style and presentation. But; that doesn't define who I am as a person.

Get to know me, the person inside, no matter my sense of style. Introduce yourself and chat a little, try to uncover who I am before judging me. Lend a listening ear to hear my story, before condemning me, and be a friend rather than an enemy.

Look at me; I feel pretty; pretty in my little pink dress that my mother had gotten for my sister on her birthday. I play with the neighbor's son; we've been friends now ever since we found out that we were not like the rest of the children in the area.

We hate our clothes, we hate our identities and we hate having to hide who we really are. I hate my life, I want to tell my secrets, but since we cannot comfortably live them, I want escape on the wings of a dove to a faraway land where no one would know I was born male behind the pretty little pink dress and my friend Michael was really born Melanie.

We want to be free to fall in love, we want to be respected, and we want to live our lives happy in our skin even in a society that doesn't agree to same-sex principals. I have faith in God, but how can I deny these feelings. I was a baby boy, transformed into a teenage girl and blossomed into a beautiful woman.

I am not ashamed of being born male, I am not ashamed of being trans-gender, and I am not ashamed of having emotional feelings for members of my own sex; after all, that is what I am. I'm not asking the world to become transgender; I'm not seeking to confuse the minds of those that are hetero-sexual. I'm not wishing to re-write the principals of God; I'm simply asking to be allowed to be me and be appreciated for just that.

What can I do if I feel like a woman? What can I do if I'm homosexual? What should I do if I'm attracted to woman? What should I do if I act like a man and I'm lesbian? Should I fake it; pretend or be true to who I am; a gay/lesbian/transgendered individual who shouldn't be observed any different from the rest of society?

You are heterosexual and like religion where one has that right to choose their faith, I respect you. However, I'm a human being who is not imposing or deploying my lifestyle on you, I simply ask that you respect me, leave me alone and allow me to live my life true to who I am, what I am and to whom I love.

Here I stand a product of greatness; I walk in the footstep of respect and honor. I'm the neighborhood boy who grew into a man that sits in the company of presidents, kings and queens. I'm the compassionate individual who walked the hallway of hospitals and held the hand of broken, sick, bedridden hurting persons when there wasn't a crowd watching and cameras recording.

I'm the generous giver who gave anonymously to charities that feed the hungry, clothed the naked and sheltered the homeless. I'm the person who stood in the gap for disadvantaged disenfranchised children and parent them with love, passion and care when men allowed themselves to be nothing more than sperm donors and women were too caught up in their busyness to be mothers.

I am that friend who always answered the phone day or night when persons called in need of my assistance. I gave all that I had to those that were in need and even to some that were in greed. I gave the shirt off my back, the pants off my ass and even the drink from my lips. I've blessed with my time, my concerns, my home, my ear to listen to people's problems, my body of shoulders for persons to cry on, and my thoughts of advice to help persons make wise decisions.

I'm the individual who you introduced to others, including family members, close associates, friends and even foes. I'm the person you called your hommie, your brother, your friend and who you told I love you to. I am the one you took to your home and allowed me to hung out with you and your family members. You boasted about me, you addressed me as your best friend, your brother and someone you appreciated being in your life, and that's great and I'm grateful being a part of your life as well, we've been through thick and thin and managed to get out wearing smiles on our faces.

However; why things changed when I welcomed you into my personal world of secrets and revealed to you that I was gay/lesbian/transgendered? Aren't I the same person? To me, nothing has change except for the exchange of knowledge and my deception of who I pretended to be in your company. Was all that not real?

Throughout my life I've heard people refer to lovers of the same sex as "Mentally sick people, nasty, freaks", and the lists goes on of graphic fraises called out of people's names. They were beaten, rejected, disrespected and disenfranchised by opportunities, and some were even killed as a result who they loved.

As a child I was verbally abused by homosexual slurs though I didn't knew what the words were. I was disrespected and refused opportunities as a result of my skin color. I was molested at the age of three by a man in his mid twenties, molested by family members and friends and finally molested at fourteen by a man in his mid-forties.

I was a poor disenfranchised barefoot boy who walked the streets of the out island to most places without shoes as a result of my parents not being able to afford enough shoes for different purposes.

If we are going to categorize homosexual lesbian transgendered persons as people that are "Nasty, mentally ill and freaks", then we should also label everyone else with problems with the same names, which doesn't exclude much of anyone.

People of all different race caliber and financial status, from all walks of life, once drunk or high of illegal substances the "Nasty freakish mentally ill character jumps out of them and introduces itself to a civilized environment that is considered normal.

An individual who abuses substances such as drugs and alcohol, once on the product and out of a controlled state of mind, they do things most would never imagine or expect to be unveil out of persons that may have been known to lead respectable lives viewing them in a normal setting, and to me, that is considered "Freakish and nasty".

For one to allow themselves to get drunk to the point where they are found sprawled out on the floor of barrooms or drug houses wet and soil from their own waste is beyond nasty and freakish.

A mother have to be mentally ill to allow her child/children to be sexually abuse, neglected and mistreated by persons they know and whose identity they wish to protect. Men that beat their wives, molest his children and neglects his family is truly a mentally ill individual.

Poverty may be hard to endure, without question. However, riches is a gift chosen for a hand picked few. Though everyone wants wealth, it is not meant for everyone to have. Many of whom that are in possession of wealth were not mentally qualified to possess it, and without elaborating further, I ask that you reflect your minds to the pages of history and those whom were destroyed as a result of uncontrolled wealth. Nonetheless, it is nasty, cruel and freakishly silly for possessors of wealth to make fun of the poor and disadvantaged.

I can go on forever highlighting points that would validate my statement that if homosexuals, lesbians, and transgender persons are people with all sorts of problems, then aren't we all?

The difference of who we are is what makes us uniquely special in our own way. Poor people are different from those that are rich. African descendents or Blacks are different from those that are Caucasian or whites. The Hispanics and Asians are uniquely made to distinguish their differences from other races. Even the drunks are different from those that are sober.

Homosexual and lesbians are different from those that are heterosexual. Bisexuals are different from those who desire one specific sex. Transgenders are different from those who believe they were born correctly, and Trisexuals are different from those who just aren't sure. However you look at it in whatever category you welcome yourself in, differences is what we are and collectively, we maintain a balanced world.

I have my personal take on things, but whether you are a drunkard, poor, a homosexual transsexual or bisexual, rich, black or white, Asian Haitian or Hispanic, I respect you just the same and appreciate you for your differences.

I will conclude by saying that if we look around our communities, there are people dying, mothers and children hurting and struggling in attempt to get through life; there are wars and rumors of wars. Our streets are at ankle length with blood that came from the bodies of our children. Prisons are overcrowded with children who will become adults in captivity. Hospitals are turning patients away as a result of not having room and facilities to doctor their issues. Suicide is at its peek, but searching for that edge to go yet a step further. The question is:

When will we stop the bigotry and hate? When will we stop the bloodshed? When will we stop boxing people in houses of whose better best and not so go to worst? When will we realize that the riches were giving to us to feed the hungry and clothed the poor without cameras recording to testify our deeds on earth? When will we spread love to those who rather run to the valley of dried bones than to seek our hands of help? When will be live and let live?

As a brother of the human race I beckon, plead and beg you the community to stop the violence, stop the hate, stop the bigotry, stop the bloodshed and stop the bullying of others who may same considerably different. You don't have to love or like them or their differences, but you can respect and leave them alone.

Respect each other's differences and focus on issues that we can systematically combat to make this world a better place. Poverty, homosexuality, drunkenness, and all the other acts have been here since the beginning of time and they will continue to be here as long as this world breathes fresh air into another morning's dawn. Let us learn to practice the attitude of love, life, acceptance and respect to and for each other.

This is my special prayer.

LAST NIGHT THE CLOUDS CRIED!

Teardrops fell from each teary eye,
Sadness rained from dark gray skies;
Last night I watched clouds cried.
As one more part of someone died,
As one more soul was laid to rest,
One more mother cried, as one more family was put to a painful test.

Precious one, how your clouds cried,
Precious one, I feel your pain inside.
Precious one, no more walks, no laughter, no hugs,
Precious one, untimely and senseless, went the one you loved.
As one more soul was laid to rest,
One more child is considered blessed.
As one more family is put to the test,
One more heart is relieved from stress.
As one more ocean wave flow like the tide,
Sadly, it's one more cloud that has to cry.

I felt like weeping, and sometimes did,
I watched your weakness, through the strength you hid.
For your encouragement, I prayed in the midst of the storm,
Dear to my own heart, as if my own son.
The wind blew strong, with pain and anger,
What once shine bright like the sun, the seas suddenly calmed her.
Untimely and senseless, went those we loved,
Cursing instead of blessing, was exchanged for kisses and hugs.

WITH THESE CRYING EYES

Faith; "That is the substance of things hoped for". It was the substance I held on to when the weight of the world was rested upon my shoulders and those I had depended on the most abandoned me. The world seemed to be against me and apparent friends became my enemy.

My home was my hiding place; I was petrified to go outside, because I didn't want to be seen by the enemy. Fear fed unhealthy thoughts to my mind, which then walled my body into my own prison. To be spotted in the distance or walking the streets was my sacrifice.

I did not want to die, but thoughts of death attempted to reside into my mind and many days and nights I held on to my pillow and painfully cried until I became ill from not eating, due to the abundance of hurt that stole my appetite.

The four walls of my home became the prison that I had gotten use to after days of being boxed in. Thank God for the days when my emotions took compassionate leave and pain gave mercy upon my soul, because it was at those times I found room to smile, strength to eat, and the will to socialize. I even tried fighting angry suicidal thoughts in effort to begin regaining control of my life, emotions and the person I was.

I associated myself with two that shared one house, one bed, one love, one passion, but different dreams. Although I welcomed and appreciated one as a distant friend, she had a different mindset from her mate and was too busy chasing dreams and accomplishing goals, which didn't left much room to afford me the attention I desperately needed when I needed it. The other was a close associate, but genuine trust and respect for another's privacy was something she knew nothing about. As a result, the physical time we spent together was rather brief.

I was like a convicted felon blessed with the opportunity of being released to the fresh open air and sunshine for an hour or two before being re-confined to the tiny cube they were housed in for the remainder of their sentence. Back to my apartment I went. Back to the thoughts of yesterday, while eagerly hoping for the painful cup to quickly leave my lips.

My heart was a stranger in the body which had housed it ever since the day it signified the entrance of life into this world then twenty five years earlier. I fell onto the bed and like hands that was idle and vulnerable, my mind drifted away into the archives of my life's history.

The further my mind drifted, the painful the thoughts became. The painful my thoughts became, the more depressed I got. The more depressed I got, the weaker and unconcerned I became about the importants of life. I literally lye in bed watching as life was passing me by.

The more I had endured, the longer it seemed to take, and like a pipe that is filled to its capacity, yet pressured to take in more, I burst into tears.

With these crying eyes I reflected back to the day when I was about three and a dirty young man in his late twenties stuck his penis into my mouth due to my being poor and disadvantaged.

Poor and hungry, standing at the road's edge with my fragile hand stretched out begging for loose change to be freed from the burden of hunger; he capitalized on the opportunity to molest me.

With these crying eyes I thought of an evening when I was five going through the entire day on an empty stomach in anticipation of my mother providing food for me after getting home from a day of washing and ironing people's laundry. But, to my disappointment, she brought nothing. I thought she had forgotten that she hadn't left anything earlier that morning, so I walked into her bedroom and found her in tears on the floor crying out to God for Him to provide her something to put on the table to feed her babies.

With these crying eyes I reflected back to the almost three years I spent in the house of the Finleys, my adopted family. I was around seven when they asked my mother to have me lived with them where shortly after I was beaten and verbally abused almost daily for no reason other than them refusing to take responsibility for their own actions and face their problems. But rather, they used me as a beating bag and a computer to store their manuscript of insults and verbal bashings. However, due to fear of what lies would be told to my biological parents, I kept it all bundled up inside and hoped to die.

With these crying eyes I thought of being in that constant state of depression during those long years I spent with my adopted family. After being treated as a beaten bag for the family; to get away, I often escaped to my friend and neighbor's house for a bit of peace and happiness. Peace I got, but happiness, the jury never came in with their verdict.

I was about nine and he was around eight; nevertheless, I paid an awful price for that peace, which was sexually explored and violated by one I called friend. One who had to face me every day at school as we were in the same class and one who I ran to in attempt to release my heart from the abundance of painful secrets that were stored inside. But, before I got a chance to, I was used for a sexual object by him. I wondered, for the acts that he had performed and had ask me to perform on him, who was molesting him.

With these crying eyes I thought of the year I was nine and as if I was not suffering enough by the hands of my abusive adopted family members and the sexual experimentation of my body by someone I had trusted, I was again hit by grief when two of my biological brothers were ripped out of my life and sent to a juvenile prison facility.

With these crying eyes I reflected back to the few months I spent with my biological father at about ten and experiencing his violent cruel wrath to the extent where my siblings and I was forced to eat our dinner from an outside dish where stray dogs were fed.

With these crying eyes I thought back to the year I was fourteen years old and locked into my home alone with an almost fifty year old sexual predator and stranger whom deceived his way into my house after discovering I was an unaccompanied minor. In fear of being badly hurt or killed, I stood still as the monster took pleasure in massaging and caressing my private parts.

With these crying eyes I thought of being nineteen and living on the streets. I slept in abandoned buildings, because I had no place else to go. My mother's house wasn't an option, because it was at that place she and others joined together to laugh and hurt me with queer jokes and insults.

With these crying eyes I thought of a day at twenty-five when one wrong decision caused me to spend thirty-six hours locked down in a filthy cold jail cell where I slept on a brick slab without a warm blanket. As if the insults from cops, being forced to urinate on the very floor I slept on, and the embarrassment of facing those whom looked up to me wasn't enough; I was compelled to endure tongue lashing from foes I thought were friends as though they never knew me.

With these crying eyes I reflected back to being in my late twenties and due to searching for that love and attention I desperately craved, I recklessly engaged myself sexually with strangers from all walks of life at times unprotected without even being concerned of their names, who they were or even what diseases they were carrying.

Reckless is an understatement; I guess I'm being modest to the factual way I really was living my life just a year or two ago. As I lye and reflected back to those days, indeed, I could not helped, but to cry.

It took me awhile to get over what I was going through. However, when my eyes had exhausted all the tears I had to cry and the river I had cried dried up; I was able to smile again. I regained value and self worth. I took back the strength I once had when those that were around me utilized my kindness as a sign of weakness to their advantage.

I found the will to forgive those that had despitefully used and abused me mental and emotionally, the genuine friendship I had offered, and my generosity. But, it took that experience to open my eyes to the reality of brief existence.

I understood and accepted the fact that those individuals were only in my life for short periods of time, and for whatever reason, after they had accomplished their goal and deposited the ingredient into my life, whether good or bad, they had to leave. Yet, I kept holding on to them. Therefore, God had to reveal their identity before they had destroyed the man he needed me to be.

I separated myself from them all, found new friends, fought hard and begin rebuilding my life and relationship with Christ Jesus, who developed a better stronger wiser me.

The experiences I went through growing up I would not wish upon my worst enemy. However, I have no regrets and I'm grateful to have gone through it all. I took responsibility for my actions, changed what I could have, and those I couldn't, I gave up to God for Him to work on.

I'm a better man today as a result of my past, and rather than beating myself over the head for mistakes and bad decisions I've made, I will use or rather I am using what Satan meant for destruction and allowing God to help and direct me to places and the lives of those, especially youths that can be renovated and rebuilt.

As I have shared in the body of this book, we pass people as we daily navigate through the journeys of our lives; and like me, some are seen carrying a smile, while others seem to be broken. Nonetheless, that outer expression might be a deception; therefore, we must be extremely careful of what we say to and how we treat them, because we don't know what baggage they are being force to carry and a few positive or negative words can either breathe life or death to that environment, and "The life you may save or take, may be your very own".

In this book, my first independent release, I've shared many stories of others, and this; no doubt, is another. However, this particular story is a glimpse into the life of me, the author, and if it helps if only one, then the experiences

I have experienced is more than experiences, they are gifts and blessings to a developing world.

A MOTHER'S REGRET

Don't let me be broken please God,
don't let my retribution depend on him taking his life.
I'm sorry my child, I was young when I had you and didn't know much about
parenting.

I wish I could tell you how much I wish I had died by your side.
Laying here with visions of your death,
laying here viewing pictures of me standing above looking down upon you
asleep in that casket.

I frequently have nightmares of you taking your life, and it frightens me, because it seemed as though I was standing right there watching you do it.
The night I took your life by means of neglect, will be a pillow of encouragement for me to make a change in others for the mistakes I've made.
Please don't hold me responsible, I'm broken already my child.
My heart is so broken; I wish I could have turn back the hands of time to do
things differently.

I'm so sorry I can't take it back, and above all that has happen, that is what
hurts the most.

FROM MY HEART TO YOURS!

Sometimes it takes a while to appreciate the things that we don't want to accept. But, eventually we usually do. It is strange to think about how we change from caring so much about something, to finally letting it go, to eventually erasing it from our thoughts.

It is a long gradual often painful process, but the outcome is rewarding. In the beginning of the letting go stage, it is especially difficult. This is when change is at the most drastic. The old habits, beliefs and hopes are shattered and we're forced into a world of unknown instability.

At first, this new environment is terrifying, maybe even depressing. However, over time it becomes more and more familiar to us. After enough time we realize that we are resilient enough to survive and that we're capable of being contented with the changes, it is all left to a matter of adaptation.

Things change and we change with them. Sometimes it is personal growth, depression, lifestyles and gender, races and creed; a general evolution that doesn't make us any worse or better as individuals. Hopefully, we're observant enough to keep ourselves constantly learning and growing.

The only thing that could prevent us from changing is we attaching ourselves to the past and denial of the new. The power of denial is a strong toxic that keeps us imprisoned in the past and we remain infants in a maturing world. What a stagnant and horrible place to waste our lives dwelling in.

Nonetheless, there are plenty of people who spend years holding on to past habits, beliefs, and hopes regardless of the signs of change. Sometimes, living with denial and being unhappy with what they have is easier to hold on to than it is to deal with fears of uncertainty.

If most people were to leave their prison of denial and ignorance as it relates to the acceptance of differences, they would have to confront their disappointments, loneliness and work toward learning how to survive in a different environment that is opened to change. The thought of doing such a thing can be so overwhelming that people would chose to remain in their cell of stupidity rather than to venture out.

Yes, accepting change and adapting to something new can be frightening; maybe even terrifying. But, it is worth it to sacrifice the prospects of something new and amazing in order to emancipate our intellect from comfort zones of the past we know and cling to.

Difference is very important and we all deserve the right to live our lives differently if that is what we desire to do. Those who wish to be loners have that right. Others who desire to dress themselves and have their heads shaved differently from the rest of the public should be accepted for their choice of style.

Homosexuals, Transgenders, cross dressers, lesbians, bisexuals and Tri-sexuals are all people who deserve to live their lives respectively in any community as long as they aren't breaking laws and imposing on others.

The way I look at it, as long as that difference, no matter what it is, is not robbing others of their education, bashing and teasing children with racial words of hate and bigotry, stealing from the pockets of poor hardworking others, and taking people's lives, then that difference should be welcome and embrace, because if we eliminate difference in our society, we will be eliminating artists, writers, movie producers, doctors, lawyers, lecturers and college professors, teachers, presidents, world leaders, poets, lovers and friends.

What possibilities are you foregoing for the sake of holding on to the past or not accepting one's choice of lifestyle, one's choice of religion, one's given complexion, and one's disadvantage? To answer this question, please don't quote the Bible, because Jesus said "Let he without sin cast the first stone, and love thy brother as you do yourself".

This world is not perfect, but it is balance and I know that there will always be persons who would continue to practice intolerance, school shootings, display the language of hate and bigotry and commit suicides as long as this world breathes fresh air into another day for the fact that we are living in a world of sin. Nonetheless, we can minimize the number of lives that are being affected as a result of pettiness and ignorance.

We cannot stop the existence of life, though others violate people's rite to live. We cannot stop the sun from shining or the rain from falling, only protect our skin from being burnt or wet. We cannot prevent hurricanes or earthquakes from visiting and or destroying our land and properties, because they are beyond our control. However, we can prevent the amount of destruction done by protecting our things and taking heed to warnings issued by meteorologists and vacate ahead of time.

There are far too many things going on in this world today that is beyond our control, but is directly affecting our lives and it is unnecessary for us to be intentionally adding to them.

There is the fall of the economy and teens entering society with a kinder-garten level of education; there are hospitals that are closing doors on little girls that had matured to mothers before completing junior high school, there are crimes and poverty, wars and rumors of wars and all the other day to day troubling issues.

There are thousands of innocent lives that are being sacrificed daily for the safe keeping of an unborn generation; yet it is this generation that is ig-norantly killing each other, bashing others with slurs, beating and violating people as a result of their identity; all for the sake of fun and humiliation, disrespect, and because they could.

For the sake of our unborn; parents need to be better role models; the law needs to implement programs that will work to help keep our neighborhoods safe for our youths and people. Principals, teachers and faculty members must implement programs that will take action against intolerance and exe-cute harsh penalties for those who practice them. They all should be properly train so that they can identify silent problems and recognize signs of bullying and intolerance, rather than waiting for the violent aftermath.

We should not allow the behavior of a few to sacrifice the lives of many innocent others. I hope you care enough about yourself in the long run to realize that maybe it's worth it to accept change. But, then again; maybe you have good reasons for holding on to the past.

There is a fine line that is drawn between what we should hold on to and what we should let go of. Maybe there's still some hope of things becoming what you'd like it to be. If this is the case, then best wishes. If this isn't the case, then do what it takes to move on and accept the change and look forward to the future.

TO THE FALLING ROSE PETALS

I trust that beyond the abuse, there's presence.
Beyond the pain, you can find healing.

Beyond the falling ends and broken parts,
You'll find forgiveness and loving hearts.

Beyond the tearful eyes that dropped a river of crying shame,
You'll find laughter, joy and capability to smile again.

Beyond the silent raindrops and brokenness,
Your body finds strength, and your heart discovers wholeness.

Beyond the pain, abuse and hell you were given,
Your soul finds faith and the gate of Heaven.

THIS 21ST GENERATION NEEDS 21ST MINDS, LEADERS; A GOVERNMENT THAT CARES!

We elect presidents, prime ministers and other leaders with a team of supposedly intelligent people to govern our land with the best interest in mind for the people. I personally believe and have often reminded persons that there is a leader for every generation, because that principal individual would not only have an understanding of the way the generation thinks, but also be fully equipped with the knowledge and resources to lead them.

For the thirty years that I have been alive, I have never voted in my country or for any political figure for that matter. Why? Because, upon many other issues and their deflating strength of honesty, I couldn't support leaders from the Nineteenth Century whom have given all that they could have to the country, and with nothing left but knowledge, they want to continue to lead youths of the Twenty-First in an age where most of them don't even know how to turn on a computer or address issues that really affects teens.

The Commonwealth of the Bahamas is in the condition that it is as a result of exhausted leaders whom realize they have nothing more to give to the country as it relates to strategies of wealth, safety and problem solving skills, but for greed, they give a little to manipulate the people to get a lot.

When we look the status of where our country is at and the widely spread fear that is obviously painted on the faces of our people; fear of spending the next dollar as a result of not knowing where the next will come from or if they would have a job to return to; fear of walking out of their doors and being shot down like dogs in the street, and fear of the direction the country is headed; with not much comfort coming from the government officials, we all are like ships that is racing toward a stormy weather without forewarnings.

Too long we have been allowing political figures to get away with a fraction of their responsibilities and manipulating people into continued support to office. They act is though they have the best interest of the people at heart when they don't.

I cannot speak for leaders of other nations, but those that have lead and continues to lead the people of the Bahamas, with exception to the earlier builders like the late greats Sir. Pindling and others of his time, people just stop caring about people and pride themselves on simply getting riches.

A few decades ago when we were an unknown collection of islands respected men and woman fought and broke barriers so that Bahamians could live in a country that is independent and married to its own identity. "United we stand, divided we fall", that was the mentality they carried with them into their offices and topics they spoke of at the round table of world leaders, which eventually deleted thoughts of separation and divide, uniting Nassau to Ne Providence where citizens became free to dwell and own properties in locations equally to other natives of race.

What happen to the people who fought actually cared and allowed citizens to walk into their offices to share painful secrets that were privately dealt, allowing people to eat bread and afford housing for their families?

What happen to leaders who fought shopkeepers and prevented them from skyrocketing food prices, allowing poor people to continue to feed their families? What happen to the leaders who separated themselves from their offices weekly to walk through run down communities highlighting issues and addressing them to the best of their abilities?

Where are the government agents who allowed doctors and Medicare to concern themselves about people's lives and health first, and payment secondary? Why are they allowing people, their people, and the people of the country of their ancestors to suffer and live the way we are?

They have stopped caring about their people and that is very wrong, because we have no other identity but that of a Bahamians and others of their native lands. Where can we go and who can we run to if we cannot lean on those we have supported into office?

The late Sir Lynden said in an interview before he died that it is important for the citizens of any country, as natives to own a piece of the land of their heritage, because he said, if you don't, you are a citizen of one that posses the land, even if they aren't from the country. Yet, leaders of today have made it next to impossible for ancestors whom have worked their fingers to the bone for all of their lives and died without owning a piece of property to will to their children.

I'm proud, but sometimes I am ashamed to know that I am a true Bahamian, given the fact how we are often disrespected and brushed off as if we don't deserve better from people who should have understood difficulties as their mothers and fathers were once in our shoes.

I don't endorse the behavior of my youthful brothers and sisters who give it all up to rob and terrorize others, but what else can they do when they have done all they can the right way, but are ignored and deceived by those they opened up to and trusted. They don't care about us, they really don't, I don't care what garbage they may try to dump into our minds.

If these government bullshitters really did care about us, the people, do you think they would allow the crime rate to be at the ridiculous level that it is?

If the government was properly governing the land in the best interest of the people, today there wouldn't be the vast amount of senseless murders each year and allowing crimes to become an adopted member of our families, the community and country.

If the government had the best interest of the people at heart and respectfully managing our land, people would not be overwhelmed with fear to the extent where they sleep at night with weapons in their beds as if they are lovers and mates and would rather rest comfortably in their homes like infants of innocence.

If these clean cut robbers that were hired to govern our land genuinely cared about people and were in control of issues facing the people, families wouldn't have to be island hopping, neighborhood jumping city crossing, state relocating and country migrating all in attempt to discover peace, security and happiness.

Our people are obsessed with locking doors and checking windows, afraid to get out of their vehicles to enter their homes at nights or they alert neighbors before getting out, and are considering vigilante justice as a result of a government that is sitting by and allowing injustice and murder to climb.

Legal law breakers are those governing our land and the criminals are those that are in control of it, because they are the ones living comfortable lives and manning our streets, stalking and preying on our families, while law abiders are living in fear.

I cannot speak for other countries, but for decades the people of the Bahamas' colony of islands were and continue to be disenfranchised by the government. The rich persists to advance into wealth, while the poor diminishes to the hurting.

Former and current Members of Parliament are in possession of more land than they could ever utilize in a lifetime, yet they persists in making it extremely difficult for hardworking members of society to get five hundred square feet of property even in the most low line areas.

Parliamentarians whom have served less than a complete term in government have moved from modest homes to mansions as a result of becoming millionaires dishonestly from the wealth that was created from the backs of hardworking citizens who sweat through the years and paid their taxes.

Through the years the citizens of the Bahamas has suffered as a result of un-marital affairs of then serving Parliamentarians that were photographed at the bedside of a late celebrity whom had gotten special privileges; others were caught in cars sexing members of society behind the backs of their wives; two were asked to resign their term for fighting in the House of Parliament, another allegedly fathered a child with a teenage school girl, despite him being old enough to be her grandfather and had his wife, while others abused their authority and utilized moneys that were intended to better the country for the people to fund personal business deals.

However, but unfortunately, despite all that the citizens have gone through with these reckless averagely respected persons, they remained loyal to them and continued supporting them again and again to office. Yet we are those they continuously neglect, brush off, disrespect and pimp to poverty.

But; when will we learn and begin to hold these well dressed criminals of authority responsible for their actions? Why are we allowing them to continuously manipulate and take advantage of us? When will it stop being a battle between parties and political divides and become a nation of Bahamians and other country men and woman that believes we deserve better than what is being thrown at us. The result of us focusing on parties has and continues to cause us to suffer greatly.

I do believe that the best gift or legacy one can ever give or leave is the "Gift/legacy of service" and to serve in honor. People should be obliged to serve others and when given an opportunity to carry out that responsibility, responsible members should take advantage of the chance to represent the people with the highest degree of respect, gratitude and dignity. They should fight for them and issues confronting persons that are hurting as if they were fighting uninvited terrorists invading on their private spaces.

Despite what the haters may say, thank God for the United States of America, a country that is today being lead by a man with a history of hardship and roadblocks. He is grateful and understands if not for his father's scholarship, his presence would have been unknown.

As a former community fighter for people's rights, he had limitations when he wanted to give more to the people. As a Senator he had restrictions. But, as a man holding one of the highest most powerful offices in the world, this is his time to open up doors that were slammed shut for decades in the face of race as it relates to hate.

This is President Obama's time to spread the wealth around to run down communities and do things he was restricted of doing when he turned down corporate opportunities of first class salaries to walk the street with little old ladies and single mothers that were loosing their homes.

This is his time to answer the call of Hurricane Katrina victims who have yet to exhale from the devastation that has held them captive and poverty stricken ever since waters washed away family members, opportunities and dreams; leaving them defenseless in a country where its then President's mother looked down on the poor and spoke from lips of unconcern inhumane thoughts.

This is his time to clean up the streets of Chicago, New York, Detroit, and all the other major cities and ghetto like communities where violence and poverty hits home, fight for the youths of his city, fight to have programs implemented that would serve as housing facilities and warm welcoming places that will entice teens to stop the violence and increase the peace in society with buildings that is designed by bullets of automatic weaponry and genuinely give care and concern to hungry mouths and homeless bodies.

God has humbled that nation to elevate a man who shares my skin color and passion to the highest office to be a voice to mouths that have been wide-shut for decades. I beckoned you Mr. Obama to open doors of opportunity to the hurting people of your country that will serve as an encouragement for them to want to truly be proud Americans. After all, they are the people who introduced you to the pages of celebrity; they are the people who wrote your name in the Genus Book of World Records, and they are the people who gave you your voice. Will you today, return the favor and be theirs???

This Twenty-First Century generation requires a Twenty-First Century intellect and mindset of leader and I'm grateful that this modern bracket has matured with an independent mindset and refuses to allow these robbers to manipulate them with their sugarcoated bullshit and instead, focuses their time on issues and the strength of one's character and legacy.

The first black American President, Mr. Barrack Obama, my idol ran his campaign on the slogan of change and it is that "Change", after poor less fortunate persons had suffered, were disenfranchised and left behind, people gravitated to and supported, despite the party they were members of. That is the change I want to see in the Bahamas and ask that persons in countries all over the world support.

As we approach the next general election in twenty-twelve, I'm hoping to see and be a part of a political team of people to enter the arena of government with an entire new way of thinking, a different attitude of governance and those who are not power hungry, money greedy and persons that could appreciate the gift of service to the disadvantage.

I want to see an unselfish government who will fight for the lawful and not the lawless. I desire to support and be a part of a group of persons that will create opportunities and jobs that will help people to feed their families with food, afford colleges and bring dreams to life instead of rehearsed speeches and broken promises.

I also want to live in a nation under the authority of a government that cares and would fight equally for all people and their problems, but especially for issues that relates to abused victimized children and senior citizens.

I know as it relates to the dishonest tattered legacy, which those before had left, this may be a lot easier said than done and might take awhile for the people to lend us their sense of trust, but I have no doubt in my mind that it can be accomplish if we pride ourselves on being a people that is passionately concern about people more than profits.

Change I believe in and we can certainly make change happen if we choose not to be like the rest. I was grateful to live to witness the magnitude of change come to life on November 4th, 2009 when Mr. Barrack H. Obama was supported into the office of the presidency after decades of ridicule, hate, bigotry, discrimination, setbacks and abuse that were carried on the backs of blacks; I pray to see the day supporters of the Free National Movement (FNM), the Progressive Liberal Party (PLP) and all the other disenfranchised persons of this and all nations would unite to demand better and more from persons before and after they take office.

I want them to reject stagnant unproductive long serving agents of the same and support character, respect and the embodiment of compassion and care for people. If we do, I promise we will have a better country to live, because we are all in this together and the decision of one affects us all.

LETTER TO THE PRESIDENT/ PRIME MINISTER

Dear Mr. President/Prime Minister:

"Violence in our country is horrific", is there a solution?

The very late great composers of our National Anthems wrote words of entrance and blessings, which with intent, to alert the world of not only the birth of a special nation, but also of the quality of its citizens. Poet Francis Scott Key wrote, "God bless America, land that I love". Bahamian great Timothy Gibson asked his fellow Bahamians, which I'm a proud one, to "Lift up our heads to the rising sun, Bahamaland, march on to glory with your bright banners waving high".

Oh how sweet to sing such powerful words with pride and joy as we watch our beautiful flags flow from side to side in an atmosphere where black men and black woman are free to be comfortable in their own skin, dwelling under the umbrella which the creator Himself lives and breathes, as it is often foretold by the humble world renown scholar himself, Dr. Myles Munroe, whose also from this nation.

Today I often ask myself if these are the same nations Mr. T. Gibson and Mr. Scott Key wrote about; the countries Sir. Sidney Poitier and Dr. Mya Angelou speaks of and humble little old ladies dream of.

Violence is threatening the welfare of our small, yet great and greater nations, and though this truly breaks my heart, what is even more disturbing is the fact that we are allowing it to be taken directly from under our feet by thugs, domestic terrorists, and those who came into this world to be destructive forces.

Haitians are dying by boatloads risking their lives to get to the Bahamas for a better way of life. Jamaicans are giving all that they have just to be able to afford an airfare to get to this nation; in blind faith, believing once they get here safely, they will survive. Cubans are risking their lives escaping from a communistic iron-fist dictator just to smell the fresh air that blows through the trees of the American states; the land self proclaimed of the free.

They are giving their lives so that members of their families can, if only get enough to eat. However, we fortunate Bahamian and American natives can call these great nations our homes and don't have to run or risk our lives to get here, because it is already ours. As I look at these differences, I hang my head down in shame, giving the fact that my own are those that seek to destroy me by the decisions they make from day to day.

Mr. President/ Prime Minister are you really reading the stories in our published papers on your drive to the office each morning, or is it just another story that captivates your attention for a mere second, before your mind refocuses your eyes to the beautiful structures neatly built along the boardwalks?

Did the murder of Corporal Dion Bowles meant anything to you; does it take any effect on your day to day life?

Did the recent murder of soon to be father, Devon Bethel woke you out of your sleep the night members of the law enforcement body riddled three bullets into his slender body?

How about the life of Mr. Strachan who was violently taken from this world as he drove up to his house, leaving behind a wife and family?

Mr. President did the murders of little Caley Anthony, Heiley or baby girl Sandra Cantu rekindled that no tolerant fire for rapists and killers of babies?

Maybe it was the fallen teens that were killed in Chicago, Detroit, Los Angeles and Miami that disturbs your nightly rests?

I guest, just maybe the mother whose fighting for her life in the hospital after being shot in the face only seconds before a vehicle of six precious jewels and a father was shot at, resulting in a few injuries; maybe that sent up a red flag alerting you that violence is at our doorsteps and if we don't work quickly, death will walk into our homes and become all of us. After all, these offenses transpired only days within each other.

Mr. President/Prime Minister the burning question is, who do we run to when we are steering down the barrel of adversity? Who do we talk to when we cannot speak at all? Who do we tell our secrets to when secrets isn't easy to share?

The attitude of law enforcement agents are molding and pushing good boys to go bad. They condemn you first, disrespect and treat you like an animal before your guilt or innocence is proven. So by the time innocence is proven, by the way you were treated, you really want to commit the act or another to revenge the inhumane way that you were handled at the hands of those that should respect you.

Who do we go to for counseling when pastors, teachers and advisers are molesting and sexing our children? Who do we run to when police officers are holding fifteen year old boys and girls unknown to relatives in prison beating and raping them even to the point of death?

Who do we call on for protection when it is police personnel that is harming us, breaking into homes and stealing our hardworking items of sweat? How can we continue to eat bread and feed our families, especially in this time of recession when storeowners are blatantly taking our advantage overpricing food? Finally, how can we even consider being a friend to the police when they aren't friends, law keepers and protectors of innocence?

Mr. President/ Prime Minister if these real life stories don't give you sleepless nights and morning hangovers, then I really don't think the position you're holding is the right one for you, for when you consumed the responsibility of Chief Executive Officer of this nation, the burden of your people rests upon your shoulders and if little old ladies have to sleep at nights with pepper spray under their pillows in fear for their lives, while you sleep like an infant, then that position is not for you.

Mr. President/ Prime Minister the son of a member of your staff, Mr. Lesley Miller was graphically snatched away a few years ago, and the many American politicians that were murdered; of course, a father and the law should do whatever it takes to bring justice to those whom violated the right of those to continue living.   However, I must ask, is the justice system for one and not for all?

Is it only for the rich and powerful of these nations and not those that are poor and weak? How about for my cousin Edward Harris who was killed and thrown into a canal when he had just begun to live, or my young friend and mother Travonne McKinney who was stabbed to death and taken from her daughter at twenty-two? What about the murder of Chad Conrad Clarke, a gay young man who was hacked to death and thrown into bushes?

We don't need to spend millions of dollars boosting up security on our borderlines to protect ourselves from terrorists Mr. President/ Prime Minister, because they are living right on our soil. If one can threaten the welfare of its nation, then I don't consider them my own and because of it, we should not hesitate to prosecute them to the very extent of the law.

There are many domestic terrorists living on our soil that is threatening our livelihood by means of violence and they must be stop, caught, killed and prosecuted.

It seem as though we are birthing and grooming terrorists from every dimension.

Students are carrying weapons to schools to harm other students, and as we reflect on the history of the educational system, there are more society rejects than there are those who can read at kindergarten grade level. Children often threaten the lives of adults and if action isn't taken, we often find juveniles committing heinous offenses.

Mr. President/ Prime Minister I have already lost a number of family members, friends, and classmates to violence and honestly; it may come as the norm to others, but I'm all cried out. I don't think I can take anymore of this bloodshed. Something must be done, because I don't want to have to ask permission to violent offenders just for the right to walk the streets of a country I inherited from my ancestors.

I don't want to be one that has to run from my own country to others in order to sleep with both eyes closed, and I sure don't want to have to arm myself with a weapon to fight for a land that God freely gave to me.

Mr. President/ Prime Minister, solutions call for changes and in order for us to discover solutions we must accustom ourselves to changing our way of living, our lifestyles, and the way we have accepted the normality in which we live and breathed.

God is watching us and it is high time for the cover-ups, the friendships, and the overlooking to cease. The God you often speak about in speeches is the same God I serve. If we don't weed out those that have no respect for His laws, then the rocks will cry out and do it for us.

In conclusion Sir, I must ask that you reflect your mind back on those days of the recent hurricane season; God gave us a fair and complete warning, but we laughed in His face after covering us with His hands of protection. As a result, He removed it, called the hurricane back, if only to show us that he is God and beside Him, there is no other.

Violence no doubt, frustrates us; yet, day after day we continue to live going about our daily routines, even if we do it in fear. My solution to this problem is; if I may give an idea to the government of these great nations, it would be to in fact, serve this country without compromise, without friendship, and with an iron, but fair fist.

Execute justice to the greatest extent of the law, no matter who the individual or individuals are breaking them. I understand you cannot do everything, but if you make an example out of one, others will know if one plays with fire the consequence for their action is getting burn, and they will be burnt.

I once again will quote the Bahamas very own world-renowned motivator, Dr. Myles Munroe who informs us, and I quote; "There are four types of persons living in this world:

(a) Those who watch changes take place.
(b) Those that change themselves because of change.
(c) Those that refuse to change.
(d) Those that make change happen".

If the hazard of violence in our day to day lives frustrates us, then my question to you is; which part of change will you allow yourself to continue to live and breathe there in for the sake of your people?

CONCLUSION

As I look back over my life, it is clear to me that any success I have and does gain can be attributed to my outlook on life. I have never lost hope in my future. It is my mission in life and my calling on this planet to impart into others the belief that we can choose to live a life filled with hope, peace, kindness and brotherly love, because anything is possible if we believe and we are willing to work hard to get it.

I have never lived a life of regrets. I'm attempting to use every event that has occurred in my life as a learning experience. However, there are things in life, had I known how to handle them back in my earlier years, I would have dealt with them completely different, even if things would have turned out the same.

If I knew then what I know now, I would have been able to see various situations and life experiences from varying perspectives. I am certain that the lessons for me would have been greater.

You can benefit from the lessons I've learnt along the way. Even now, I still have no regrets. Would I have done some things differently? Sure.

I can tell you that I spent far too much time worrying about people and what they thought of me. I know for sure that I would have loved myself sooner and removed certain toxic people from my space eventually.

In fact, I would never have allowed them into my life in the first place. I would have spent zero time doubting myself. I would have made my health a priority. I would have lived in the moment and approached life one day at a time instead of always living for the next step or goal that was to be achieved in my life.

I would have spent a great deal of time laughing and not carrying around hurtful feelings. I would not have been so hard on myself and given myself permission to make a big deal about it and more mistakes along the way. I would have talked less and listened more.

I know now that I loved a great deal and although I was not always loved back, because I loved, I am a better person for it. I know now that I'm a true risk taker and although everything I have done has not always worked out the way I would have liked it to, taking risks helped me to appreciate how much I could trust and depend upon me.

I know now that putting my others first has had long lasting returns, because when all the dust settles it is my gift of service that gives me joy like no other.

I now know that when you truly can forgive you empower your life in ways unimaginable. I know now that everything happens for a reason and that trusting in God fills any hole that was in my soul. I know now that turning my life over to God completely is the best thing that has ever happened to me.

I also know that happiness cannot be found outside of me. I know now that money is not everything and that it truly cannot buy peace of mind. I know now that life is meant to be lived to the fullest and it must be lived with fewer, if any, regrets.

The object of my writing this book is to inform, educate and strengthen the ability of the weak; to guide and direct them into a better way of living, as well as to question the decision in which we make for our daily lives that may directly affect others enjoying theirs.

For many years of my life as a teenager I was mentally, physically, emotionally and sexually abused by those whom suppose to love and protect me. My advantage was taken; I was beaten, sexually abused, bullied, hated and pushed around by class and schoolmates, family members, friends and members of the community, which forced me into a state of depression, resulting in isolation for the most part of my life.

During that painful period of my life, it opened my eyes and made me questioned my future as to whether accomplishing goals for my personal benefit were more important than for me to help point another less fortunate child into a direction of the stars, whom may have never seen one shine.

I stopped, looked and listened to what their hearts were crying out in great detail and discovered factual findings that the media body has fed our teens with negativity, entice and lure them into a mindset of the "The get now, kill or be kill, I'm representing my manhood, and the rich quick scheme, because I must have". They then overlook their stories of what take place behind the scenes in what is labeled as "The Ghetto", as a result of its philosophy.

Innocent children are rapidly becoming target practices for soldiers, beating bags for gang members, toys for sexual predators, vehicles for drug lords, and a piece of meat for street walkers and rapists.

This drove me to the point of realizing that enough was enough and one life was far too much. I could no longer wait for someone else to take a stand; I had to step up to the forefront, be the change I want to see in this world and make an example, using my life as a template.

God had made me to realize very early in my life that he had called me for a special purpose; whenever I were to open my mouth, even then, it usually captivated the attention of people, compelling them to stop, look and listened to what was being said. Although I was unaware of it then, I realize he was molding me for a time and purpose such as this.

I experienced my fair share of struggles and hardships, troubles and trials, pain and heartaches, which hurt me at times, being faced with difficulties. However, I had to feel what futured and fueled my career and calling.

My message had to come, not only with experience, but also with sacrifice. It had to be authentic; therefore, I have no regrets, because if I hadn't experienced it, then it would have simply been opinions of empty words without meaning. My tears were making room to accommodate and heal many bruised and battered hearts and emotions.

The sounds of innocent voices are screaming for help, and it is not as though they are not being heard, but because listeners are choosing to ignore them. The very stone on which they lay and the walls of our communities that continues to be painted with innocent blood has now become alive; they are telling stories, pleading for their help, and attempting to get our attention in bold red blood stained banners.

I hope this book helped motivated you, the reader and propel you to partake in making a difference in another person's life, especially a child. I also hope your knowledge had increased by what was said throughout these pages, make a great impact and change in your life.

DEDICATIONS

This book is dedicated to both shooters and victims of every high school that was affected by violence in America and around the world. It is also dedicated to the memory of Travonne Alisa McKinney, Edward Brandon Harris and everyone whose lives were shortened by violence in the Commonwealth of the Bahamas.

Special thanks go out to my guiding light; my mentor, friend and father-figure, Dr. Davidson L. Hepburn; my parents Mr. and Mrs. McDonald Ellis; my adopted mother Mrs. Cestina Finley; my spiritual parents Barbara and Michael Griffith, Brother Carl Farquharson; my three best friends Kenny Taylor, Reynard McDonald and Gaston Farrington; my four brothers Ernest, Andrew, Romeo and Mario Ellis; my beautiful nieces and nephews in the Bahamas and the United States; St. Andrew's Presbyterian Kirk Church youth group, Omar Newton, Soul Seekers and everyone who has touched my life, if only by an encouraging word or gesture.

A very special thanks to the great team at Trafford Publishing Company, the staff at the Bahamas' Ministry of Education, Career and Technical Section, Administrations and the office of Mr. Ralph Bowe, and all who had helped making this project a success.

Thanks for your support.

God bless.

Author